SEVENTH WARD

BAYOU
ST. JOHN

31

Esplanade Ave

18

22

St Claude Ave

N Broad St

32

33

TREMÉ

23

17

N Galvez St

MARIGNY

BYWATER

N Claiborne Ave

N Rampart St

Basin St

FRENCH
QUARTER

Mississippi River

9

ALGIERS

CENTRAL
BUSINESS
DISTRICT

WAREHOUSE
DISTRICT

38

Luther King Jr Blvd

39

10

TRAL
TY

25

LOWER
GARDEN
DISTRICT

Esplanade Ave

Governor Nicholls St

2

1

N Rampart St
St Ann St
Orleans St
St Peter St

Bourbon St

4

3

Chartres St

5

Decatur St

GARDEN
DISTRICT

Magazine St

6

34

35

37

24

36

iana Ave

40

41

IRISH CHANNEL

7

8

N Peters St

Canal St

5th St

Westbank Expy

MW00475235

COCKTAIL BARS

1. Cane & Table
2. Bar Tonique
3. Pat O'Brien's
4. Jewel of the South
5. Peychaud's
6. French 75 Bar
7. The Carousel Bar & Lounge
8. Beachbum Berry's Latitude 29
9. The Sazerac Bar
10. Barrel Proof
11. The Columns
12. Restaurant and Bar at The Chloe
13. Vals
14. Cure
15. Twelve Mile Limit
16. Revel Cafe & Bar

LIVE MUSIC

17. d.b.a.
18. Kermit's Tremé Mother-in-Law Lounge
19. Banks Street Bar
20. Maple Leaf Bar
21. Tipitina's

NEIGHBORHOOD SPOTS AND DIVE BARS

22. Other Place
23. Little People's Place
24. Chart Room
25. Sportsman's Corner
26. Brothers III Lounge
27. Le Bon Temps Roule
28. The Kingpin
29. Roberts' Bar
30. Snake and Jake's Christmas Club Lounge
31. Pal's Lounge

RESTAURANTS

32. Willie Mae's Scotch House
33. Dooky Chase's Restaurant
34. Brennan's
35. Napoleon House
36. Tujague's
37. Galatoire's
38. Compère Lapin
39. Pêche Seafood Grill
40. Molly's Rise and Shine
41. Turkey and the Wolf
42. La Petite Grocery
43. Brigtsen's Restaurant

CURE

CURE

NEW ORLEANS DRINKS
AND HOW TO MIX 'EM

NEAL BODENHEIMER
AND **EMILY TIMBERLAKE**

PHOTOGRAPHS BY DENNY CULBERT

ABRAMS, NEW YORK

Contents

INTRODUCTION

Have you noticed that whenever you mention New Orleans—it doesn't matter where in the world you are—people's faces light up? I've traveled all over, and whether I'm in Bali or Budapest, when I mention my hometown, even complete strangers get excited. "New Orleans! Big Easy! Mardi Gras!" And then they will raise an imaginary glass to their mouth and take a fake drink—the universal symbol for New Orleans.

Then comes the fun part of the conversation, where I get to say that I actually work behind bars and own a couple of cocktail spots in the city. Being a cocktail guy from the cocktail capital of the world is a great way to make new friends.

As a native son of New Orleans, I can tell you that a lot of what you've heard about my city is true. Yes, we sometimes walk down the street sipping cocktails from plastic cups—they're called go-cups, and it's perfectly legal. Yes, a random parade might erupt in the middle of your commute home from work—it's probably a second line, so you can either sit there and wait in traffic or hop out of your car and join the party. We really do love jazz (the annual Jazz Fest draws 450,000 attendees), and we really do eat king cakes at Mardi Gras (but never at any other time of year).

We're known for being a fun-loving food town . . . with a bit of a drinking problem. And there's definitely some truth to that! But there is also life beyond the French Quarter and so much more to New Orleans than television shows and tourist guides will tell you.

Today, ours is mostly a tourist economy, sustained by the 18 million visitors who descend on the city each year to ride the streetcar down St. Charles Avenue and engage in questionable behavior on Bourbon Street. But what many people don't realize is that when my family, the Bodenheimers, settled in Louisiana in the 1850s, New Orleans was the fifth most populous city in the U.S. (In the 1840 census, it was the third, after New York and Baltimore.) That may seem crazy to modern readers, but it's true. New Orleans was a major, cosmopolitan city and an economic capital before it was a cultural capital. It was the gateway to the Mississippi and the American Midwest, and like all great port cities, it was home to immigrants from all over the world who exchanged goods, cultures, and traditions.

I mention all of this because I think it is important context for understanding the *real* New Orleans, not the Disney version. And it will help you better understand our crazy, fascinating, and unique drinking culture, which could only exist here. New Orleans was once a French and Spanish colony with special access to imported European goods like brandy and absinthe; a thriving port and depot center where barges of whiskey from Kentucky docked near ships filled with rum and sugar from the Caribbean; and a merchants' town where people made decent money and were happy to spend it in the city's many coffeehouses and drinking establishments.

I'm a bar guy, not a professional historian, but around here most bar guys know a lot about history. In part, this is ego—we consider New Orleans to be the "cradle of cocktail civilization," and we want people to know it! (Without New Orleans, there would be no Sazerac, no Vieux

Carré, no Ramos Gin Fizz—and none of the thousands of modern cocktails that those drinks inspired. You're welcome.) The cocktail may not have been invented here, but it wouldn't have flourished the way it did without us.

I love and am very proud of my city's history, but I don't want you to get the wrong idea about me. I am not one of those "mixologists" who wears suspenders and old-timey clothes, and I don't have a waxed mustache. My bars and restaurants—I co-own four of them in New Orleans—are definitely modern affairs. In fact, my first bar, Cure, which opened in 2009, was the city's first modern stand-alone craft cocktail destination. Since then, other craft cocktail bars have opened here, and many of them are great. But we were the first.

Our mission upon opening was the same as it is today: to walk the line between old and new, to run a bar that honors New Orleans's past while inventing new cocktails that are the classics of the future. We have worked to create a bar that represents what New Orleans is really about.

Yes, we revere the past. But we are also constantly rebuilding and reinventing ourselves—out of necessity, since we have suffered so many catastrophes, from the Great Flood of 1927 to Hurricane Katrina in 2005 to the recent devastation caused by the coronavirus pandemic and Hurricane Ida.

In New Orleans, we are defined by the relationship between preservation and progress, and the pendulum swings back and forth between the two. When Hurricane Katrina made landfall in August 2005, my world changed (although not nearly to the extent that so many others' did). I was living in New York at the time, working as a bartender at The Modern by Danny Meyer. In a single moment, I suddenly knew I wasn't where I was supposed to be. I can't explain it, but if you were from New Orleans and didn't live there anymore, you knew the city you loved needed its sons and daughters to return.

In the years that followed, New Orleans struggled to rebuild what was lost. But we also talked a lot about the *new* New Orleans and what the city could be if we all started looking forward a little more. That is where I got the idea for Cure. I realized that a city that reveres the cocktail as much as New Orleans does deserved a *modern* craft cocktail bar—a place where old-timers could come in and order a perfect Sazerac, made with quality rye and a beautiful, hand-cut garnish. (In the early 2000s, these were hard to come by except in a few old-school bars.) But also a place that felt cool and modern rather than from another time, where young people who maybe didn't know much about cocktails would feel comfortable and excited to explore new drinks. I wanted to apply everything I had learned in New York—about proper technique, the importance of good ingredients, and the wider canon of classic cocktails—to create a bar that walked the line between preservation and progress.

There are many ways that we honor the past at Cure. For one thing, we always have an array of classic cocktails on the menu, and especially New Orleans classics like the Sazerac and Vieux Carré. We have dedicated years of our lives to mastering these recipes, studying the history, tasting every relevant modern product that comes to market, and field-testing techniques and specs until we find the recipe we think is perfect. Call me arrogant, but I think we make the best Sazerac on the planet.

In addition to the classics, we always have a rotating cast of modern seasonal cocktails on the menu, invented by our brilliant bar staff. But we've set some parameters for ourselves: Each of these cocktails has to be a riff on a classic cocktail template. In this way, we strike a balance between old and new and ensure that our drinks are always firmly grounded in history. Our bar isn't pretending to be some nineteenth-century relic, but it doesn't do postmodern molecular mixology, either. Like New Orleans, it has one foot in the past and one foot in the present.

It's been years since Cure first opened its doors, and a lot has happened in the interim. In 2018, Cure won a James Beard Award for "Best Bar Program." That year, I also became the co-chair of the Tales of the Cocktail Foundation, which organizes the largest and most influential cocktail festival in the world (see page 165). My business partners and I have opened more bars and restaurants in New Orleans. There's now a Cure outpost in the New Orleans airport, Cane & Table in the French Quarter, an agave-focused bar and restaurant called Vals, and a bar called Peychaud's in the building that Antoine Amédée Peychaud (page 24) once lived in. In 2021, we partnered on our first location outside of New Orleans, an ambitious restaurant called Dauphine's in Washington, D.C.

I'm also the father of a bright and beautiful daughter, and I'm lucky to count my wife, Kea, as my partner in life and business. Kea is a lawyer and founder of the Sherman Law Firm, a boutique shop where she advocates for people and small businesses in our community, as well as the founder of Sherman Strategic Affairs. She is, quite simply, one of the best people I know, and she has brought a new level of sophistication to Cure. I am well aware of how lucky I am.

Cure has been open for well over a decade, but in New Orleans, a decade is like a blink of the eye. I've always wanted for Cure to stand the test of time and be here long after I'm dead and gone. With each year that goes by, we're a bit closer to that goal.

But recently, amid the tragedy and chaos of the coronavirus pandemic and Hurricane Ida, I've begun to think about how my job as a hospitality professional extends beyond just welcoming people into my bars and restaurants. At Cure, we've always considered ourselves stewards of the New Orleans cocktail legacy—innovators and keepers of the flame. Now, with so many wonderful establishments on the brink, it seems more important than ever to write things down, to chronicle everything that makes modern New Orleans so great. Hopefully this book is a step in that direction.

ABOUT THIS BOOK

Over the years, as so many of the leading bars in the country published cocktail books of their own, folks kept asking me when the Cure book was coming out. The notion seemed crazy to me at first—I was still convinced that I was going to end up living under a bridge, trying to figure out how to pay off my debts, rather than becoming a published author.

But the more I thought about it, the more I realized that something was missing in the world: a book that celebrates New Orleans's *living* cocktail culture—the modern spirit of the city. I'm a bar guy, so the best way I know how to tell this story is through cocktails.

I like to think that the one hundred-plus recipes in this book represent New Orleans's past, present, and future. Of course they include the classics every self-respecting drinker should know, especially if you're from New Orleans—the Sazerac, Julep, Vieux Carré, Ramos Gin Fizz, Cocktail à la Louisiane, and French 75—plus some underappreciated gems like the Pequot Fizz and Roffignac. Then there are new cocktails invented by our all-star bar team: the Howitzer, a bourbon-based French 75 riff I created for our very first menu that people still order today; the Black Flamingo, a cold-weather tiki cocktail by Alex Anderson; even a Hurricane that is brilliantly updated by Kirk Estopinal with premium rum and a house-made fruit syrup (and no hangover, when consumed responsibly).

Cure couldn't exist without our amazing community, so I've also featured some friends in these pages. My childhood schoolmate Katy Casbarian talks about the opening of her now-legendary Arnaud's French 75 Bar. Writer and photographer L. Kasimu Harris talks about the city's disappearing Black bars and lounges and what we can do to preserve them. Musician and New Orleans funk royalty Ian Neville shares his favorite spots to grab a drink and listen to live music. I've even tapped some of the city's most iconic chefs, including Frank Brigtsen, Nina Compton, and CureCo.'s own Alfredo Nogueira, to share recipes for New Orleans–inspired snacks to enjoy alongside a drink.

My greatest hope is that many years from now, readers will flip through this book and be transported to one of the most vibrant and exciting moments in New Orleans's cocktail history. I really do believe we're living in a new golden age for drinking. In New Orleans we are preservationists by nature, and I am excited to put a little something in the historical record that shows that New Orleans drinks are still some of the best in the country nearly one hundred years after Prohibition.

CURE'S HOUSE STYLE

SPIRITS

Nearly all the recipes in this book call for specific brands and bottles of a spirit. This is based on how we develop recipes for our bar: We're constantly tasting and assessing new products to figure out how they'll work in our cocktails. For example, our Sazerac recipe (page 29) calls for Sazerac-brand rye. In the beginning, we chose this product for practical reasons—when we opened in 2009, there just weren't many ryes on the market, and the Sazerac Company was sitting on quite a bit of beautiful six-year-old rye. So it was a natural choice to use this local product for our Sazerac. Since then, Sazerac rye has gained a following and has therefore become harder to find. (In most markets, it's allocated, but not in New Orleans.) But we still use Sazerac rye because we love its rich roundness and its spice, which makes it particularly well-suited to Old-Fashioned–style drinks.

This is just one example of how we choose spirits for our bars. Our decisions are based on a lot of factors—taste, aesthetics, price, availability—that might not matter as much for you at home. If you can't find a recommended bottle, you can substitute a different product; just know that your result will be a bit different than ours. Where possible, try not to stray too far from the category of spirit, though. If a recipe calls for a London-style gin, stick with that rather than a New American style, which is significantly different. Don't sub an aged (añejo) tequila if the recipe calls for a blanco.

ICE

At our bars, we are blessed with dedicated ice machines that take our municipal water, filter it, and convert it into crystal-clear 1¼-inch (3-cm) cubes or crushed pellet ice. We use the 1¼-inch (3-cm) cubes not only for serving, but also for shaking and stirring, which helps us control dilution and minimize ice deterioration.

I would be very impressed if you had a professional-grade Kold-Draft ice machine at home. So I advise people to invest in several silicone ice molds. Buy 1¼-inch (3-cm) molds for shaking, stirring, and serving and 2-inch (5-cm) molds for drinks that are served over one large rock. Use distilled water to get your ice as clear as possible. If you really want to go for gold, you can fill a little Igloo cooler with water, freeze it to create a giant ice block, then chip away any imperfections with an ice pick. The nice thing about this approach is that impurities will gather in one area of the ice block, which means once you chip away the cloudy parts, the ice is clean and clear. From there, you can hack off pieces of ice as needed for your drinks. (Personally, I love the way these irregular hunks of ice look; they make every drink unique.)

To make crushed or pellet ice for juleps, cobblers, and the like, take several handfuls of ice, wrap it in a clean, lint-free dish towel, and release your inner caveman. Whack at it with a rolling pin, mallet, muddler, or kitchen spoon until the ice is crushed to your desired size: finer for lower-proof drinks, a bit chunkier for boozier drinks. If your Secret Santa gifted you one of those canvas Lewis bags that are designed for crushing ice, my advice is to use it once and then throw it away. We used to use them but found they are impossible to clean well, and the seams always get moldy because of all the dampness.

A few recipes in this book call for cracked ice, which is somewhere in between cubes and crushed. To crack ice, start with one of your 1¼-inch (3-cm) cubes, hold it in your nondominant hand, and whack it with the back of your barspoon. This should crack it into anywhere from two to five smaller, irregular pieces.

FROM LEFT TO RIGHT

Use silicone molds to make large cubes for serving over one rock

Crushed aka pellet ice

Smaller 1¼-inch (3-cm) cubes can be used for stirring (pictured), shaking, and serving

A FEW TECHNIQUES YOU SHOULD KNOW

DOUBLE-STRAIN: I talk a lot about consistency (at this point, it's basically my mantra) and a big enemy of textural consistency in cocktails is ice shards. They can just completely change the mouthfeel of a drink. This is why for all of our shaken drinks, we take the added step of straining them through a fine-mesh strainer into the serving glass.

DRY-SHAKE: This is the technique we use for all of our egg- and dairy-based drinks. If you make as many Ramos Gin Fizzes as we do, you will become intimately familiar with the dry shake. Basically, you combine ingredients in a shaker *without ice* and shake until well integrated—typically about 30 seconds, or until you can hear that the liquid in the shaker has stopped sloshing and you can sense that it has been converted into foam. Then add ice and shake again until the cocktail is chilled and diluted. In many instances (our Ramos Gin Fizz, for example), you'll add ingredients in stages to maximize and stabilize the foamy meringue layer that floats on top of the drink (see page 160).

MUDDLE: Say it with me: Muddling is not murdering. Too many people, even professionals, just whack the shit out of their ingredients when they're muddling. This is no good, especially if you're working with fragile herbs like mint. Pound too aggressively and you release unpleasant chlorophyll flavors into your drink. Think of muddling as *pressing*, not pounding an ingredient to release its flavor. For mint and other fresh herbs, I don't even use a muddler; I use the back of my barspoon and press the leaves against the side of the mixing glass. For smashes like the Chamomile Kilt (page 138), which involves muddling a citrus half, I press down with the muddler and rotate my wrist (imagine turning a doorknob) three times, just until the citrus oils are released but not so hard that the bitter pith gets extracted. When I'm muddling whole fruits or vegetables, like a strawberry or cucumber, I go a bit harder, since my goal is to get the ingredient close to pulverized so that when I shake it, it integrates with the rest of the liquid.

WHIP-SHAKE: Whip-shaking is similar to dry shaking, but here we add one or at most two cubes of ice to our shaker tin along with the other ingredients. We often use this technique for lower-proof drinks that will be served over crushed ice. In this case we want to activate and foam the ingredients but do not want to add too much dilution, since the crushed ice dilutes it already.

FROM LEFT TO RIGHT
Double-straining, shaking, muddling

GARNISHES

A few basic guidelines when it comes to garnishes: Make sure whatever you're using is fresh and well-washed. At Cure, we always cut our citrus garnishes to order to ensure they're as fresh as they can be. (Precut citrus makes me sad because you lose all the wonderful citrus oils.) When you're shopping for lemons, keep an eye out for the ones with a craggy surface and big pockmarks. These ugly ducklings are actually great for garnishing because they contain a lot of oil. Here is an overview of the styles of garnishes you'll see in this book.

CITRUS PEELS: When a recipe calls for a citrus peel, you should use a Y peeler to cut a wide swath from the surface of the fruit, trying to minimize the amount of bitter pith you cut away.

CITRUS WEDGE: We don't garnish with citrus wedges very often because we prefer to carefully calibrate the acidity levels in our drinks rather than have a guest squeeze citrus into their own drink. However, some guests request a citrus wedge. In this case, we cut off the top and bottom ends of each citrus, then cut the remaining fruit into longitudinal eighths. Trim the top of the wedge, remove any seeds, and cut a small notch in the center of the wedge so you can affix it to the rim of the glass.

CITRUS WHEEL: Slice your citrus through its equator into wheels ⅛-inch (3-mm) or thinner. I love to use a mandoline to cut my wheels as thin as possible so that I can float them on the surface of the drink rather than mounting them on the rim of the glass.

RIGHT

Brandy Crusta (page 110)
with horse's neck

OPPOSITE

Chink in the Armor (page 33)
with pigtailed twist

FRESH HERBS: Contrary to what you may have heard, generally you should not "slap" fresh herbs like mint, unless you're planning to use a single leaf. To activate a mint sprig or bouquet (which is just several sprigs), grab the mint by its stem and kind of flick or rub the leaves against the back of your hand. Your goal is to activate the aromas without bruising the delicate leaves. If the recipe calls for one or two leaves, then you should place the leaves in the palm of your hand and flick (or lightly slap) the leaves with your finger pads (don't smash them in between your palms; that's too much force).

HORSE'S NECK: Use a Y peeler to cut away the entire peel of your citrus in one long spiral. Then, coil it along the interior of your serving glass and, if desired, allow the top to drape over the rim.

PIGTAILED TWIST: While holding your citrus near the drink, use a channel knife to cut a short, 3- to 4-inch (7.5- to 10-cm) skinny string of peel. As you cut, citrus oils should spray over your drink to season it. From here, you have a few options: You can tie it into a knot, coil it into a tight spiral (although this, to me, is very 1990s/2000s), or just coil it loosely and affix it to the rim of your glass.

HOW TO EXPRESS CITRUS

Many of the recipes in this book instruct you to express a citrus garnish before either mounting it on the rim of the glass, inserting it into the drink, or discarding it. The logic here is that we want to enhance the aroma of the drink by getting some of the fragrant citrus oils to stick to the exterior of the serving glass, and by extension, the hand of the drinker. That way, every time a guest raises the glass to take a sip, they get a nice whiff of orange, lemon, or grapefruit oil. (This is one reason why we use unscented hand soap at the bar.)

To express a garnish, hold it lengthwise in both hands between your thumbs and index fingers, with the surface of the peel (not the pith) facing outward. With the peel aiming downward at the glass from above, gently squeeze your fingers together so that the pockets of citrus oil spray over the glass. If you're working with high-quality citrus and a peel that you just cut, you should be able to actually see the spray. Reorient your hands so you're aiming for the left side of the glass (9 o'clock) and squeeze the peel a second time to spray that side of the glass, then reorient your hands again to hit the right side (3 o'clock). Dab the peel on the edge of the glass that is farthest from you (12 o'clock) to make sure you have consistent coverage.

Some bartenders will tell you to rub the citrus peel along the rim of the glass, but we do not recommend this. We want consistent coverage over the surface of the glass, and the best way to achieve this is by aerosolizing the citrus oil. For the same reason, we prefer using an atomizer to apply rinses to the interior of a glass.

At this point, your garnish should still look nice and presentable—if it doesn't, you're squeezing too hard. From there you will either discard, insert, or mount the garnish.

OPPOSITE, TOP TO BOTTOM

Spritzing a "rinse" from an atomizer

Bitters, decanted into eyedropper bottles

EXPRESS AND DISCARD: Express your citrus, but do not place it on or in the glass; throw it away. This way, you get a bit of that citrus essence but not too much.

EXPRESS AND INSERT: Express your citrus, then insert it into the drink, typically between the ice and the edge of the glass.

EXPRESS AND MOUNT: Express your citrus, then carefully rest it on the rim of your glass. Sometimes fate intervenes and our mounted garnishes fall into the drink somewhere between the bar and your table. But I kind of like letting the universe have its say as to where the garnish ends up. If you lose a mounted garnish into your drink at home, it's definitely not the end of the world.

DROPS AND DASHES, SPRITZES AND SPRAYS

Most of the recipes in this book call for you to apply bitters in drops rather than the more typical dashes. Although most commercially made bitters come in dasher bottles, we take the extra step of decanting our bitters into glass jars topped with a medicine dropper, which allows us to more precisely control the amount of bitters in each drink. This is for two reasons: One, the size of the dasher-top aperture varies from brand to brand, which means that the volume of a dash is never really consistent. Two, for science- and gravity-related reasons, the size of a dash from a single bottle varies depending on how full the bottle is. Drops from a medicine bottle are a more consistent unit of measure. If you don't feel like going to the trouble of decanting your bitters, seven drops is roughly equal to one dash, so you can just do the math for each recipe.

"Spritz" is another unit you'll see pop up in recipes, typically for absinthe, bitters, or any other substance that is applied to the interior of a serving glass or surface of a drink to create

aromatics. You'll want to buy an atomizer—you can find plastic versions at any drugstore since they're used as travel bottles—and transfer the ingredient in question to it. A spritz is one spray from the atomizer. We prefer this approach rather than the more traditional "rinse," which involves pouring a small amount of spirit into the serving glass, rolling it around to coat the interior, and then dumping the excess. We find this wasteful and also imprecise; rinses vary from bartender to bartender, but four spritzes is always four spritzes no matter who is doing the spraying.

GLASSWARE: TO CHILL OR NOT TO CHILL?

In this book, whenever a drink is served up (no ice), the instructions say to serve it in a chilled glass. To accomplish this at home, carefully arrange the glassware you'll need in your freezer at least thirty minutes before you plan to serve the drink. But this is one place where I'm not going to be totally dogmatic, and I will tell you that it's really up to you whether you want to chill your glassware or not.

The common wisdom behind chilling glassware has to do with thermodynamics: If you're stirring your cocktail to your desired (cold) temperature but then pour it into a room-temperature (or, worse, dishwasher-warm) glass, the heat of the glass will transfer to the liquid inside and your cocktail will warm up really quickly.

But ice-cold isn't always the ideal serving temperature for a cocktail—and that's when the "to chill or not to chill?" question gets a bit more complicated. The human palate is not designed to taste optimally in really cold environments. This is why wine drinkers care so much about serving temperatures and why most will tell you that it's a bad idea to serve wine too cold. Riesling is a perfect example. When you sip a Riesling that is ice-cold, all you get is acid and sweetness;

there's no nuance. But as it warms up, that's when you experience all the things that make this wine great—the subtle floral and citrus aromas, the minerality, the mouthfeel.

The same principle applies to cocktails, but with cocktails, you also have to take proof into consideration. If a drink is spirit-heavy and very alcoholic, the volatile compounds will dominate and make it harder to pick up all the nuance. So with a boozy drink, a bit of chill will help mellow out the aromatic esters of the spirit and make the drink more balanced.

To my mind, there is a relationship between the ratio of spirit to modifier (bartender-speak for a lower-alcohol component like vermouth or liqueur) in a drink and the ideal serving temperature. When you're working with modifiers like fortified wine (e.g., vermouth, sherry), think of them like you would any other wine: The more you chill these ingredients, the more closed off and hard to perceive they become. I have a friend who loves to drink his Manhattans at cellar temperature (that's about 55 to 59°F [13 to 15°C]), and I think he's got a good point. I don't want *all* of my Manhattans like that, but I definitely appreciate the way the sweet vermouth shines. That got me thinking about martinis and how equal-parts or inverted (meaning, more vermouth than spirit) martinis actually benefit from being served warmer, so you can really taste the wine. Before you freak out, I will say that if it's a dry martini (meaning, a lot of spirit and very little vermouth), I am going to serve that cold as fuck. But that goes back to my original equation—the higher the proportion of wine to spirits, the warmer (or more accurately, the closer to cellar temperature) the drink should be.

When you're deciding whether or not to chill your glassware at home, you have plenty of considerations that don't factor in for us at the bar—freezer space, prep time, etc. But you should also think about what's ultimately going in the glass and at what temperature it will really shine.

CH. *1*

BITTERED SLINGS

Sazeracs, Old-Fashioneds, and Other Strong, Stirred Drinks

This chapter contains several MVPs of the New Orleans cocktail canon: namely, the Sazerac, Mint Julep, and Ojen Cocktail. What these drinks have in common is that they are all slings—which is a very early style of cocktail composed of spirit, sugar, and water—and they all have bitters. So, *bittered slings*.

Today, most bartenders would call these drinks Old-Fashioned variations. The Old-Fashioned is a category of cocktail defined by the combination of spirit, sweetener, dilution, and bitters. But I decided to go with the more antiquated term "bittered sling," in part because "Old-Fashioned" is a relatively new name for this style of drink. When Jerry Thomas first included a recipe for a cocktail of whiskey, sugar, and bitters in his 1862 bartender's guide (the first cocktail book of its kind ever published, and a sacred text for us bar people), he called it a Whiskey Cocktail. It wasn't until a decade or two later that drinkers started calling for cocktails in the "old-fashioned" way, which meant unadulterated by "improvements" like absinthe or curaçao. By the time the name Old-Fashioned came into play in the 1870s and 1880s, people were already drinking plenty of cocktails made with spirits, sugar, and bitters that went by different names. "Bittered sling" might not exactly roll off the tongue, but to me, it encompasses all of these early drinks and their modern offspring.

All you really need to know about the drinks in this chapter is that they are descended from the earliest cocktails, and they are delicious. I love bittered slings for their clean, direct flavors. This is a cocktail format where your base spirit's quality, age, and weight really matter. Can the bittered-sling treatment mask a lower-quality product? Yes, but the resulting drink never quite shines the way you want it to. A subpar spirit can always get cleaned up in a bittered sling, but you can never make a great bittered sling with a subpar product.

COCKTAIL TELEPHONE, OR:
HOW COCKTAIL MYTHS ARE MADE

If you go on a New Orleans history tour with a guide who is more concerned with lore than facts, you may hear one of a handful of frequently repeated New Orleans cocktail myths: 1) that New Orleans is the birthplace of the cocktail; 2) that the cocktail was invented by Antoine Amédée Peychaud (of Peychaud's bitters fame) and that it was a sort of proto-Sazerac; and 3) that the word "cocktail" itself originates from the name of the vessel (*coquetier*) Peychaud used to serve his drink to patrons.

The people of New Orleans are a proud bunch, so of course we'd like to lay claim to being the birthplace of the cocktail. Sadly, it's all bullshit. Most of the misinformation can be traced back to one source: 1937's *Famous New Orleans Drinks & How to Mix 'Em* by self-proclaimed "cocktail historian" Stanley Clisby Arthur.

Now, you're going to hear me talk a lot about Stanley Clisby Arthur throughout this book, because he wrote what was considered for many years to be *the* definitive book on New Orleans cocktails. I'm grateful to the man, and the subtitle of this book is a tribute to his.

But here's the thing about Stanley Clisby Arthur: He never let the truth get in the way of a good story. Despite having worked at the Federal Survey of Archives (a job he secured through the WPA), he was not a very good historian, nor was he a particularly rigorous journalist. You know how you read certain lowbrow periodicals and can just tell that it's all pay-to-play? *Give us some ad money and we'll write up your business.* It's featherlight journalism. Well, that's how I've always imagined Stanley Clisby Arthur. I just have this feeling that his approach was along the

lines of, "Hey, Hotel Monteleone: I'll write you up in my book if you give me a room for a week." And suddenly he's got an essay about how the great Hotel Monteleone is a must-visit stop for any cocktail lover.

Anyway, Arthur is the one who popularized this idea that Antoine Peychaud is the father of the cocktail. In *Famous New Orleans Drinks*, Arthur writes about how, in 1793, Peychaud, the descendant of French plantation owners who were fleeing the slave rebellions in Haiti (then the French colony Saint-Domingue), sailed to New Orleans and brought with him "among other scant possessions, a recipe for the compounding of a liquid tonic, called *bitters*, a recipe that had been a secret family formula for years."

Arthur goes on to explain that Peychaud, a trained apothecary, set up shop in New Orleans and gained popularity for the "potions of cognac brandy he served friends and others who came into his pharmacy—especially those in need of a little brandy, as well as bitters, for their stomach's sake." He further says that "Peychaud had a unique way of serving his spiced drink of brandy. He poured portions into what we now call an 'egg-cup' . . . known to French-speaking populations as a *coquetier* (pronounced ko-k-tay´) . . . Possibly through sampling too many of M. Peychaud's spiced brandies, the thickened tongues of the imbibers slurred the word into 'cocktail.'"

It's a fantastic story, so you'll have to forgive me for tearing the whole thing to shreds. The biggest problem is that the timeline doesn't check out. As my friend (and a direct descendant of Peychaud himself) Philip Greene proved by working backward from a death notice printed in 1883, Peychaud was born in February 1803 and arrived in New Orleans just a few years later, when he was a toddler. So there's no chance he arrived with some family recipe in hand and immediately set up shop.

Then there's the pesky detail that the word "cocktail" had already appeared in print by 1806 (most famously in a Hudson, New York, newspaper called the *Balance and Columbian Repository*). Babies say some strange stuff, but I don't think a three-year-old Peychaud was toddling around New Orleans and babbling about cocktails. So the egg-cup/*coquetier* theory is out the window.

The last claim, that New Orleans is the birthplace of the cocktail? Well, there are just too many ways to pick that apart, the simplest being that people were slinging cocktails well before Antoine Amédée Peychaud was born—per cocktail historian David Wondrich, London coffeehouses offered alcoholic punches as early as the mid-seventeenth century—and that Stanley Clisby Arthur was, to put it bluntly, a bullshitter.

So why do we keep talking about Arthur, and why am I writing so much about him here? Because, in spite of everything he got wrong, he did get a lot of stuff right. Peychaud did become a successful apothecary (his pharmacy opened in 1834), and he did invent a popular proprietary bitters. He did use those bitters to create "medicinal" potions, most famously a spiked brandy drink that he served from his pharmacy. Peychaud's proprietary bitters did spread throughout the city and eventually became a foundational ingredient in many classic New Orleans drinks—the Sazerac, Vieux Carré, and Cocktail à la Louisiane, to name a few. And most important of all, Arthur was the first and only person to collect the classic canon of New Orleans drinks in one place. Without his book, recipes

for the Roffignac, Vieux Carré, and Cocktail à la Louisiane may very well have been lost forever. So I can't get too mad at him for getting some of the precise details wrong. He still did me and my fellow bartenders a massive service.

In the end, I think the cocktail world can be excused for giving Arthur and his book so much credence for so many years. These days, we get ten new cocktail books published every year. But for generations, Arthur's book, along with a handful of others, was the only game in town. It was only in the last decade or so that more serious historians like Philip Greene and David Wondrich started digging into the history of the Sazerac and realized that Arthur's account didn't pass the sniff test. Reading Arthur and talking about him today is a great reminder to take everything your bartender tells you with a grain of salt. So much of our cocktail lore is based on oral histories that have been passed from one smoky, dimly lit barroom to the next over the decades. After a few whiskey drinks, even the most well-meaning narrators start to get a bit hazy on the facts.

SAZERAC

Any self-respecting cocktail book about New Orleans has to begin with the Sazerac. You'll have to forgive me for going long here, but the Sazerac really is holy water for us, so I just have to give it its due. (If you don't care about the backstory and just want to start drinking, turn to page 29).

Compared to many of the drinks in this book, the Sazerac might look a little underwhelming at first—just some pinkish-brown liquid in a stubby, stemless glass; no ice; plainly adorned with a lemon peel. Yet somehow, this humble libation became the cocktail of the city—figuratively, and as of 2008, legally. In that year, the Louisiana House of Representatives enacted a bill that named the Sazerac "the official cocktail of the city of New Orleans."* Originally, the bill was going to name the Sazerac as the official cocktail of the whole state of Louisiana, but our esteemed representatives got cold feet and didn't want to admit that we're a bunch of boozy hedonists. The city of New Orleans had no such issues.

If you read the fine print, you'll notice the bill states that the drink was "created in the nineteenth century by Antoine Amédée Peychaud in the French Quarter of New Orleans." This is a commonly held belief, especially down here, but I wish those legislators had consulted with a cocktail expert before they codified that sentence into law. An expert would have explained that Peychaud, although a damn fine pharmacist and the creator of a legendary proprietary bitters, was *not* the creator of the rye, sugar, bitters, and absinthe concoction we all know and love.

Rather, cocktail historians believe that the drink was created—or at the very least, made famous—at a saloon (or "coffee house," as it was known at the time) called the Sazerac House. Not to be confused with the present-day museum and tasting room run by the Sazerac Co., the old Sazerac House opened in the 1850s and was a combination bar and import company located on a lot between Royal Street and Exchange Place (aka Exchange Alley) in the Quarter. One of the products the import company brought in was a cognac called Sazerac de Forge et Fils, which is how the bar got its name.

The Sazerac House had a long and illustrious run until Prohibition, and then again (in a new location on Carondelet Street) after repeal until 1948. Around the turn of the century, it was the place to be. As the *Times-Democrat* wrote in 1895, "the Sazerac has for years been a favorite place of resort among the men of the city"—women were banned, there and pretty much everywhere else—"who go there to drink [*sic*] each other's health, talk over business matters or renew old associations under the influence of the delightful cocktails for which the Sazerac has such a widespread reputation. As long as any citizen now living can remember the Sazerac has been at its present location, and during all that time it has never deviated one jot from the high standard of liquids handled over its bar."

Notably, the writer makes no mention of a "Sazerac Cocktail" by name, nor do they describe a drink made with rye, Peychaud's, and sugar,

Bittered Slings

---

* For those interested in the full text of Louisiana State Senate bill RS 1420.2: "There shall be an official cocktail of the city of New Orleans. The official New Orleans cocktail shall be the Sazerac. The Sazerac, created in the nineteenth century by Antoine Amédée Peychaud in the French Quarter of New Orleans, is world known for the use of a local product known as 'Peychaud's Bitters.' Its use on official documents of the city of New Orleans and with the insignia of the city of New Orleans is hereby authorized."

served in a glass rinsed with absinthe. They do, however, note that Sazerac House bartender Vincent Miret has a "reputation as the best mixer of whisky cocktails in the City of New Orleans."

If you're trying to triangulate when and where exactly the Sazerac cocktail was invented, this last sentence is pretty interesting. Back in 1895, the term "whisky cocktail" wouldn't have referred to any old drink made with whiskey, but rather, a specific cocktail of whiskey, sugar, and bitters. An "*improved* whisky cocktail" was that same formula plus absinthe or maraschino liqueur (or both). Could Miret have been "improving" those whisky cocktails he was so famous for slinging with a dash, or perhaps a rinse, of absinthe? And might those whisky cocktails have featured Peychaud's famous local bitters? We know the Sazerac House stocked Peychaud's since 1) Peychaud ran an ad announcing his "cordial has been introduced into general use in the Sazerac House, and other principal Coffee-Houses in this city" in 1857, and 2) Peychaud licensed his formula to Thomas Handy, who took over at the Sazerac House in 1871.

"When did the Sazerac become the Sazerac?" is the type of question that cocktail-history nerds love to fight about, typically after having imbibed too many Sazeracs in the wee hours of the morning. There is always one camp that argues the original Sazerac was not made with rye at all, but rather with cognac, in the manner of Peychaud's cognac and bitters *coquetier.* Then there is another group—I count myself among them—that points out that the first known mention of a Sazerac Cocktail in print was in 1899, sixteen years after Peychaud's death. If Peychaud was calling his signature cognac-bitters drink a Sazerac, you'd think it would get name-checked *somewhere* in print. But it didn't.

What makes the most sense to me is that Vincent Miret, and after his death in 1899, his partner Billy Wilkinson, riffed on the improved whisky cocktail format until they landed on something close to the Sazerac we know today. In a stroke of theatrical genius, one of them—it's hard to say which—decided to add a dash of absinthe, which he poured into the glass, swirled, and dumped before adding the remaining ingredients. That dramatic flourish was a huge hit among bargoers of the 1890s, and was soon copied by bartenders across New Orleans.

Although there were many imitators, Miret and Wilkinson's version of the drink was the original. Over time, fans would have started to refer to the drink by the name of the establishment in which it was served: "that cocktail from the Sazerac [House], the Sazerac cocktail."

Sometime between 1895 and 1899, the Sazerac House started selling bottled cocktails. (If you assumed this was a 2020s innovation, remember: When it comes to cocktails, everything new is old.) There were six in the line, including a Whisky Cocktail, but none explicitly named the Sazerac. But the bottled cocktails, which were eventually distributed nationally, further established the Sazerac House's brand and cachet, and as New Orleans became more and more of a tourist destination, the bar and its drinks became an even bigger phenomenon.

By the time Prohibition reared its ugly head, the Sazerac cocktail was a full-blown fad. According to legend, the short story writer O. Henry (who lived in New York, not New Orleans) drank one or more every day, which to me demonstrates just how far-reaching the cult of the Sazerac really was. Its popularity took an obvious hit during Prohibition, but the true believers ensured that it was never completely forgotten, unlike so many other recipes from the golden age of the American cocktail.

I warned you I was going to go long here, and I certainly have. But I would be remiss if I didn't talk a bit about how we approach the Sazerac at Cure. In the early days, we had a lot of (good-natured) arguments about what constituted a Sazerac and how we should make our in-house version. We learned what we could about the history of the drink and used that as a guide for developing our recipe. What we all agreed on is that the Sazerac is, fundamentally, a double-aromatic improved whiskey cocktail made with proprietary bitters. What do I mean when I say "double-aromatic"? At Cure, we apply Legendre Herbsaint (a local anise-flavored absinthe substitute) to the inside of the glass using an atomizer. In this way, the anise is an aromatic, not an ingredient, that is complemented by the second aromatic, a lemon peel, which we apply to the exterior of the glass.

At Cure, we don't like a red-red-red Sazerac—we feel that if you add too much Peychaud's, it starts to taste out of balance. After many, many taste tests, we decided that 21 drops (3 dashes) of Peychaud's is optimal. But bartender Turk Dietrich, who has made more Sazeracs than anyone in Cure history, really loves Michael Jordan and started making his Sazeracs with 23 drops. Before we knew it, he had taught everybody else to do it with 23 drops, and 23 drops became part of our official recipe.

We went back and forth about whether to use white or Demerara sugar in our Sazeracs. In the beginning, I was a white granulated sugar guy: White granulated sugar is more neutral; it gets out of the way quickly and allows you to really taste the bitters and rye. But blind taste tests convinced me that the drink tastes better with a darker, less refined sugar—which, incidentally, is closer to what they would have used in the nineteenth century.

4 spritzes Herbsaint

2 ounces (60 ml) Sazerac rye

¼ ounce (7.5 ml) Demerara Syrup (page 242)

23 drops Peychaud's bitters

Lemon peel, for garnish

Spritz the Herbsaint from an atomizer into the interior of a chilled double old-fashioned glass.

Combine the rye, Demerara syrup, and bitters in a mixing glass filled with ice and stir to chill. Strain into the prepared double old-fashioned glass, garnish with the lemon peel, and serve.

IMPROVED BRANDY COCKTAIL (AKA PRE-SAZERAC)

On page 24, I spend some time debunking one of the most common Sazerac misconceptions, namely that the drink was created by Antoine Peychaud. But even Old Unreliable himself, Stanley Clisby Arthur, admits that Peychaud mixed his proprietary bitters with cognac, not rye, the spirit we now think of as integral to a Sazerac.

Even if it isn't technically a Sazerac, cognac, sugar, and bitters taste damn delicious together, and it's easy to imagine nineteenth-century New Orleanians tossing that combination back. After all, cognac was quite popular in New Orleans in Peychaud's heyday because of the city's legacy as a French colony and its special trading relationship with Europe. It wasn't until the 1860s and '70s, when a louse called phylloxera wreaked havoc on the vineyards of Europe and, by extension, the French wine and brandy trade, that cognac became increasingly rare in the United States.

It makes sense to me that once the cognac in New Orleans dried up, some savvy bartender decided to swap in rye. That doesn't discredit the idea that a cognac-based proto-Sazerac was once popular in New Orleans and that Peychaud himself may have sold a bittered brandy drink from his pharmacy on Royal Street. And so I wanted to include a cognac variation here for the history nerds out there. I call it a *pre*-Sazerac, and while it's a very different drink than a rye-based Sazerac, it's still great.

4 spritzes Herbsaint

2 ounces (60 ml) Ricou Spirits Brandy Sainte Louise

½ teaspoon (2.5 ml) Demerara Syrup (page 242)

½ teaspoon (2.5 ml) Luxardo maraschino liqueur

14 drops Peychaud's bitters

Lemon peel, for garnish

Spritz the Herbsaint from an atomizer into the interior of a chilled double old-fashioned glass.

Combine the remaining ingredients except the garnish in a mixing glass filled with ice and stir to chill. Strain into the prepared double old-fashioned glass, garnish with the lemon peel, and serve.

RIGHT

Inside Peychaud's, our French Quarter bar in the former home of Antoine Amédée Peychaud

BASIC RESHAPE

BASIC RESHAPE

TURK DIETRICH

You won't be surprised to learn that we love to make Sazerac variations at Cure. We've done a lot of them over the years, but this one from Turk Dietrich remains one of the best. "This drink was born out of a dealer's choice that I used to make all the time, a genever Sazerac," he explains. ("Dealer's choice" refers to when a guest asks the bartender to come up with a drink for them rather than choosing from the menu.) "Instead of absinthe, I rinsed with Zirbenz," an Austrian eau-de-vie made from the fruit of the arolla stone pine, "since pine works really well with the maltiness of the genever." Think of this as a Sazerac on a ski vacation in the Alps.

5 spritzes Zirbenz stone pine liqueur

1½ ounces (45 ml) Bols barrel-aged genever

½ ounce (15 ml) Bristow Reserve barrel-aged gin

¼ ounce (7.5 ml) Simple Syrup (page 243)

9 drops Angostura bitters

9 drops Peychaud's bitters

Spritz the Zirbenz from an atomizer into the interior of a chilled double old-fashioned glass. Combine the genever, gin, simple syrup, and bitters in a mixing glass filled with ice and stir to chill. Strain into the prepared double old-fashioned glass and serve.

CHINK IN THE ARMOR

KIRK ESTOPINAL

You'll see many, many recipes from Kirk Estopinal throughout the book. Kirk was the first bar manager at Cure, and by year two he had become my partner in the business. Kirk describes this drink as "a nod to malted milk balls." You'll find that a lot of his drinks are inspired by candy or dessert flavors. Even if you don't like sweets, they totally work. Genever, which is a spirit with centuries of history (think of it as a sort of proto-gin), has a strong malty flavor, almost like an unaged white whiskey. That, paired with the honey, chocolaty bitters, and honey and citrus notes from the Lillet, makes this pretty damn irresistible. (See photo on page 16.)

1½ ounces (45 ml) Bols genever

¾ ounce (22.5 ml) Lillet Blanc

½ ounce (15 ml) Honey Syrup (page 243)

14 drops Bittermens Xocolatl mole bitters

Pigtailed lemon twist (see page 17), for garnish

Combine all the ingredients except the garnish in a mixing glass filled with ice and stir to chill. Strain into a chilled double old-fashioned glass filled with ice, garnish with the lemon twist, and serve.

OLD-FASHIONED

In the early days of Cure, we called this cocktail the *old* Old-Fashioned to differentiate it from the version of the drink that our parents and grand-parents drank in the 1960s and '70s (what I like to call a "Pendennis-style" Old-Fashioned, named after the Louisville, Kentucky, club that popular-ized it). The Pendennis Old-Fashioned involves muddling an orange wedge and a maraschino cherry with some Angostura bitters–soaked sugar in the bottom of a glass, adding a splash of water from a soda gun to make a quick syrup, then topping it all with bourbon and ice.

I'm not going to claim that this retro style of Old-Fashioned doesn't taste good. It does! It's just different than what we wanted to make at Cure. We were more interested in an earlier, nineteenth-century version of the drink, which doesn't involve whole fruit or muddling. In the recipe here, I call for bourbon *or* rye, and both work. It just depends on what you're in the mood for. I'll reach for bourbon if I want a rounder, richer Old-Fashioned, and rye if I'm looking for something thinner and more spiced. Hell, you could even swap in Scotch and use honey syrup (page 243) as a sweetener, since Scotch and honey go so beautifully together. Or try an agave spirit like tequila or mezcal and use agave syrup (page 242), or an aged rum with a smidge less Demerara syrup. That's the beauty of these proto-cocktails—they are flexible and work with pretty much whatever you have on hand.

2 ounces (60 ml) Sazerac rye or Evan Williams single-barrel bourbon

¼ ounce (7.5 ml) Demerara Syrup (page 242)

14 drops Angostura bitters

7 drops Regans' orange bitters

Orange peel, for garnish

Combine all the ingredients except the garnish in a mixing glass filled with ice and stir to chill. Strain into a chilled double old-fashioned glass filled with ice, garnish with the orange peel, and serve.

COCK 'N' BULL SPECIAL

COCK 'N' BULL SPECIAL

Here's a classic that doesn't really have anything to do with New Orleans—it was created at the Cock 'n' Bull restaurant, which opened in Los Angeles in the 1930s. But Ryan Gannon, one of Cure's Hall of Fame bartenders, was always a big champion of the drink, and it really caught on for us at Cure as a solid Old-Fashioned variation. I think part of the reason people respond to it is because the brandy and the Bénédictine give it a New Orleans sensibility and shared DNA with the Vieux Carré and the Cocktail à La Louisiane. (Bénédictine, which we call a monastic spirit because its recipe was allegedly first developed by French monks, like Chartreuse, has notes of vanilla bean, baking spices, and citrus peel. It was one of those spirits imported from Europe that New Orleans took a shine to, so you'll find it in a lot of our classic drinks.) My only criticism of the Cock 'n' Bull is that it's a little richer and rounder than we generally like, so don't be afraid to add an extra dash or two of bitters to balance it out.

¾ ounce (22.5 ml) Buffalo Trace bourbon

½ ounce (15 ml) Sainte Louise brandy

¾ ounce (22.5 ml) Bénédictine

¼ ounce (7.5 ml) Pierre Ferrand orange curaçao

14 drops Angostura bitters

Orange peel, for garnish

Combine all the ingredients except the garnish in a mixing glass filled with ice and stir to chill. Strain into a chilled double old-fashioned glass filled with ice, garnish with the orange peel, and serve.

BORROWED TUNE

RYAN GANNON

Ryan had a very specific idea of what he wanted to do here—create a bittersweet Old-Fashioned with a menthol finish—so he just tinkered until he ended up with a perfect drink. His starting point was a somewhat obscure vintage cocktail called The Battle of New Orleans. "It was a total Mr. Potato Head," he tells me, referring to the now-famous process for riffing on classic templates first popularized by Phil Ward in the 2000s. (Think of a cocktail like a Potato Head doll, and try swapping in different sets of eyes, noses, or mouths—or in this case, different spirits, modifiers, or bitters.) "The main thing for me was whiskey and mint, but instead of crème de menthe, I wanted the deeper flavor of Branca Menta," which is bittersweet and herbaceous with a heavy dose of menthol.

1½ ounces (45 ml) Henry McKenna or Evan Williams bonded bourbon

½ ounce (15 ml) Branca Menta

¼ ounce (7.5 ml) Averna amaro

1 teaspoon (5 ml) Demerara Syrup (page 242)

14 drops Regans' orange bitters

Grapefruit peel, for garnish

Combine all the ingredients except the garnish in a mixing glass filled with ice and stir to chill. Strain into a chilled double old-fashioned glass filled with ice, garnish with the grapefruit peel, and serve.

CHARM OFFENSIVE

NICHOLAS JARRETT

This Old-Fashioned riff is an homage to what Nick describes as one of the greatest whiskeys ever bottled, Jack Daniel's Master Distiller #2. It's a precious and hard-to-find spirit, so if you want to use something a bit more accessible, try this drink with Jack Daniel's Single Barrel Select whiskey instead. What I love about the Charm Offensive is the hit of celery. Whiskey, peach, and celery might not sound like an obvious combination, but it really works.

2 ounces (60 ml) Jack Daniel's Master Distiller #2 or Single Barrel Select whiskey

½ ounce (15 ml) Giffard crème de pêche liqueur

21 drops Bitter Truth celery bitters

10 drops Bittermens Hellfire habanero shrub

3 drops Saline Solution (page 243)

Mint sprig, for garnish

Combine all the ingredients except the garnish in a mixing glass filled with ice and stir to chill. Strain into a chilled double old-fashioned glass filled with ice, garnish with the mint sprig, and serve.

ANTE UP

NICHOLAS JARRETT

Nick calls this his "deranged mash-up between a Stinger [a two-ingredient cocktail of brandy and crème de menthe] and a Dead Nazi [the classic dive bar shooter consisting of equal parts Jäger-meister and Rumple Minze]." This bartender's choice was created for one of Cure's best regulars, James, the owner of the terrific Freret neighborhood café Bearcat.

1 ounce (30 ml) Laird's bottled-in-bond apple brandy

¾ ounce (22.5 ml) Jägermeister

½ ounce (15 ml) Tempus Fugit crème de menthe

½ ounce (15 ml) Varnelli Amaro Sibilla

10 drops Bittermens Hellfire habanero shrub

5 drops Saline Solution (page 243)

Mint leaf, for garnish

Combine all the ingredients except the garnish in a shaker filled with ice. Shake until chilled, then double-strain into a chilled cocktail glass. Float the mint leaf on top of the drink and serve.

ELLE RIO

RYAN GANNON

This is one of my favorite cocktails, period. It kind of splits the difference between an Old-Fashioned and a lowish-proof Manhattan, with rich cinnamon notes and nuttiness from the sherry, then bitter amaro to snap it all together. Ryan and I debated whether we should reveal the true inspiration for the name of this cocktail. But I decided the truth should prevail: Elle Rio is the name of a notable Brazilian adult-film star from the 1980s. And since cachaça, a sugarcane-based rum, is the iconic spirit of Brazil, Ryan felt like the name was an apt tribute. When I asked him the backstory of this drink, he laughed and told me that he basically created it to try to lure whiskey drinkers and get them to diversify their palates a bit. His ploy worked: So many people would order two or three of this drink, rave about how much they loved the "whiskey," and then find out afterward that they were actually drinking cachaça.

1 ounce (30 ml) Avuá Amburana cachaça

1 ounce (30 ml) Barbadillo oloroso sherry

¼ ounce (7.5 ml) Varnelli Sibilla amaro

1 teaspoon (5 ml) DuBois Petite Canne sugarcane syrup

7 drops Bittermens orange cream citrate

Orange peel, for garnish

Combine all the ingredients except the garnish in a mixing glass filled with ice and stir to chill. Strain into a chilled double old-fashioned glass filled with ice, garnish with the orange peel, and serve.

FLORA ITALIA

KIRK ESTOPINAL

"This was one of my on-the-spot drinks," Kirk told me. He made it while competing in a cocktail competition hosted by St-Germain. "During one of the heats, they gave you a surprise bottle and you had to make a drink with it. I remember being a little nervous because my judge was Dale DeGroff." (If you don't already know, Dale is a total legend and considered the father of the modern mixology movement.) When Kirk was handed a bottle of pisco, he spontaneously decided to try it in a Sazerac variation, subbing it in for rye. It sounds crazy, but it worked. DeGroff loved the drink, which was a favorite on one of our earliest menus at Cure.

2 ounces (60 ml) Barsol Primera Quebranta pisco

½ ounce (15 ml) St-Germain elderflower liqueur

¼ ounce (7.5 ml) Demerara Syrup (page 242)

7 drops Angostura bitters

3 drops rose water

Grapefruit peel, for garnish

Combine all the ingredients except the garnish and the rose water in a mixing glass filled with ice and stir to chill. Strain into a chilled double old-fashioned glass and dot the rose water over the surface of the drink. Garnish with the grapefruit peel and serve.

ELLE RIO

SPICE TRADE

KIRK ESTOPINAL

Kümmel is a European liqueur that is flavored with caraway and sometimes cumin and/or fennel. In my humble opinion, many of them smell like a stinky armpit. But in the early days of Cure, Kirk took it upon himself to try to make a house-made kümmel. It ended up being fantastic. "This was in the beginning of the Rogue Cocktails concept," Kirk says, referring to the game-changing collection of drinks he and Maks Pazuniak wrote and published in 2009. Kirk calls it his "weirdo" cocktail book, but it was full of revolutionary ideas, one of which was that drinks don't necessarily have to have a base spirit like vodka, gin, or whiskey. "I love the idea of a drink where you look at the recipe and think to yourself, *Gross.* Or, *What could that possibly taste like?*" Kirk and Maks's rogue cocktails basically dared you to drink them. Adding to the mystique was the fact that Kirk's house-made kümmel looked scary: The jug of liquid with whole caraway seeds floating in it looked, at least according to Kirk, like "a million dead flies stuck in a gross brown liquid."

Now that I've definitely sold you on this drink, I have to tell you in all honesty that it's really good. Gilka kümmel is available online and in well-stocked liquor stores. Paired with the assertive flavors of Herbsaint and curaçao, it's not a subtle drink, but it's tasty.

1 ounce (30 ml) Gilka kaiser-kümmel liqueur

1 ounce (30 ml) Herbsaint

1 ounce (30 ml) Pierre Ferrand dry curaçao

14 drops Angostura bitters

Combine all the ingredients in a mixing glass filled with ice and stir to chill. Strain into a cocktail glass and serve.

YERBA AGAVE

KIRK ESTOPINAL

What a great cocktail. The Yerba Agave was a huge seller when we first put it on the menu, and it's still a crusher. Tequila, and even tequila Old-Fashioneds, are pretty mainstream today, but in 2010, they were an oddity in the U.S. Kirk's inspiration was a vintage drink called the Improved Holland Gin Cocktail, which was basically a genever Old-Fashioned. "I find aged tequilas often have a kind of dried cacao note. The Bénédictine was a way to bridge the chocolaty vibes of the tequila, and the crème de menthe adds mint but also a drying, refreshing, cooling note. When a drink is a little sweet, a touch of mint can bring it back down and make you want to take another sip." Kirk's Old-Fashioned philosophy is that the setup should fundamentally elevate the base spirit. This drink does just that: It brings out all the nuances and subtle flavors of the tequila.

2 ounces (60 ml) El Tesoro añejo tequila

¼ ounce (7.5 ml) Agave Syrup (page 242)

1 barspoon Bénédictine

2 barspoons Marie Brizard white crème de menthe

4 drops Angostura bitters

Mint sprig, for garnish

Combine all the ingredients except the garnish in a chilled double old-fashioned glass. Add ice and stir until chilled. Garnish with the mint sprig and serve.

A MOUNTAIN OF ICE:
APPRECIATING THE MINT JULEP

Some people might raise an eyebrow when I say that the Mint Julep is a quintessential New Orleans drink, simply because they associate the drink so closely with Kentucky. These are people who have probably relegated their julep consumption to Derby Day. But here in New Orleans, we're happy to sip a julep any day of the year.

Here's my argument for why we should include the drink in the wider New Orleans canon, besides the fact that many a julep has been consumed here, both today and for hundreds of years: First, the spirit we all associate with the drink, Kentucky's signature, bourbon, is a relative newcomer on the julep scene. For most of its time on earth, the julep was *not* made with whiskey; it was made first with rum, then brandy. The word "julep" is centuries old and derived from the Persian word for rose water, *gûl-ab*. In its original, medieval-English iteration, a julep was a medicinal concoction of herbs, sweetener, and maybe a little booze. But according to David Wondrich, once it made its way to Virginia in the late 1700s, the julep shed its pharmaceutical trappings and was embraced for what it truly is: a boozy party in a glass.

Notably, those colonial Virginians were making their juleps with rum. According to Stanley Clisby Arthur, early New Orleanians were drinking their juleps with rum, too: His book features a recipe for the San Domingo Julep, made with rum, loaf sugar, and mint, and suggests that it is "the original mint julep that came to Louisiana away back in 1793," brought to port by plantation owners and aristocrats fleeing the slave rebellion in Haiti. (Of course, Arthur offers no citations or evidence to back up this claim. As I mentioned on page 24, we should never take his word as gospel.)

By the early 1800s, Americans had developed a taste for imported French brandy, and more of them had the means to pay for it. So cognac became the fashionable choice for juleps. We know how much nineteenth-century New Orleanians loved their fancy European products—absinthe and anisettes, Madeira, sherry, and the like—so it seems pretty likely that they would have jumped on the brandy-julep bandwagon.

From there, a few regional spin-offs started popping up: In Georgia, South Carolina, and other peach-producing states, peach brandy proliferated in the mid-1800s, resulting in a tasty regional julep. It wasn't until well into the nineteenth century, when phylloxera wiped out the global brandy supply, that American whiskey really came into play at all.

If the base spirit is changeable, then what really makes a julep a julep? The mint, sure. But for me, it's the ice. A well-made Mint Julep is recognizable from a mile away. When you see that frosted glass with the dome of crushed ice peeking over the top, an abundant bouquet of fresh mint drilling down through its surface, you know the drink could be only one thing.

Sometimes I like to imagine those early-nineteenth-century Americans ordering their first Mint Julep. When that drink landed on the bar—when they saw that bounty of clear, cold, beautiful ice—my guess is they went totally apeshit.

We take ice for granted, but it was such a luxury back then—especially in tropical climates like Louisiana, where any ice you tasted was lake-cut in the North and transported via cargo ship down the Mississippi. On those 90- to 100-degree days of New Orleans summer, you must have been so grateful for anything that made it into your glass still frozen.

So now, just imagine receiving a tasty cup of sweetened, aromatic liquor in a silver or pewter cup that is overflowing with so much glorious ice that the exterior is frozen, almost painful to hold in your hands. It must have been such a power move to order a Mint Julep. It wasn't "Give me your most expensive bottle of wine," but rather, "Give me your cocktail with the most ice."

It is notable but unsurprising to me that the first large-scale mechanical ice manufacturing facility in the United States—some say the world—opened in New Orleans in 1868. By that time, there were several ice storage facilities throughout the city. But when blockades during the Civil War cut off the supply to precious lake-cut Northern ice, intrepid New Orleanians decided to engineer a solution. The Louisiana Ice Co. took water from the Mississippi, distilled it, and, through steam-powered machinery, converted it into ice. "The manufacture of artificial ice, at the works, is particularly attractive to the looker-on, from the fact that the operation, from the pumping of the water from the turbid river, near at hand, to the slipping out of the polished, glistening slabs of alabaster-looking ice from the tin moulds, in which they are congealed, is so excessively simple and clean," wrote the *Picayune* upon the factory's opening.

I have found no evidence to suggest that the owners of the Louisiana Ice Co. were Mint Julep enthusiasts, but it doesn't seem like that much of a stretch to imagine they were. I did find newspaper articles from the era bemoaning how ice shortages would affect Louisianans' ability to enjoy their beloved julep: "The connaisseurs [*sic*]

in good beverages and lovers of iced mint-juleps, are wondering with a heavy sigh if enough energy is left here to insure us in having ice this season. The time for such is at hand, and as yet we have not received our first hint of the Spring nectars. Who is going to move in the matter?" opined the *Louisiana Democrat* in April 1875.

My recipe on page 47 calls for bourbon, because that's what people have come to expect from their juleps. But rum or brandy wouldn't be out of place at all. The only nonnegotiable in my mind is that you must fill your glass with an overabundance of ice. At our bars, we use pellet ice from our Scotsman machine; at home, you should crack your own ice using the technique on pages 13 to 14. Add the ice to the serving glass (a julep cup is traditional but not necessary) in stages, agitating it by stirring or swizzling after each addition so it starts to melt and dilute what would otherwise just be a sweetened shot of hooch.

As you sip your icy-cold julep from a straw, close your eyes and imagine a world without air-conditioning, without refrigeration—a hot, sticky world where people rarely bathed and the smell of summer was enough to knock you dead. Stick your nose in the bouquet of mint, maybe graze that heaping mound of ice. Inhale. Is this not the best drink you've ever had?

MINT JULEP

The spec below is very traditional and very basic. So technique is important here. Despite what you may have been told, you should not "muddle" the mint. If you pulverize it, you'll extract bitter and unpleasant flavors from the chlorophyll. Instead, gently press the mint with the back of your barspoon against the glass. Do not "slap" the bouquet you'll use for garnish. Just gently brush it against the back of your hand; that's enough to activate the aromas. Add the ice in stages and agitate (swizzle or stir) at each step. Purists may scoff, but I like to add a dash or two of Angostura to my Mint Juleps. Pretty much everything tastes better with bitters.

2¼ ounces (67.5 ml) Buffalo Trace bourbon

½ ounce (15 ml) Demerara Syrup (page 242)

12 mint leaves, plus 1 bouquet for garnish

Combine all the ingredients except the garnish in a julep cup and stir to combine, making sure to gently press the mint leaves against the sides of the cup with your barspoon. Fill the glass halfway with crushed ice, then stir to agitate and dilute the whiskey. The proof of the whiskey should melt the ice pretty quickly, which is what you want—this drink needs dilution. Add more crushed ice to fill the cup again, then stir again to agitate. Refill the cup with more ice, stir one last time, then add enough crushed ice so it mounds over the edge of the julep cup, which should be frosted over by now. Brush the tops of the mint bouquet against the back of your hand to activate the aromas, then place the bouquet in the drink to garnish it. Serve with a straw.

THE OJEN CAPITAL OF THE WORLD

Throughout this book, you'll encounter the word "Ojen" and probably wonder if it's a typo. It's not—but don't worry if you've never heard of Ojen before. Even here in New Orleans, it's a bit of an obscurity.

Ojen (pronounced *OH-hen*) is a Spanish anisette (an anise-flavored liqueur) originally produced in the 1830s in the Andalusian town of Ojén by Pedro Morales e Hijo. It's hard to say when, exactly, Ojen caught on in New Orleans, but an 1883 ad in the *Picayune* proclaims "OJEN! OJEN! 50 Cases Ojen of Majorca, Superior to ABSINTHE as an Appetizer and Tonic" for sale by the distributor Paul Gelpi on Decatur Street.

I don't know much about Gelpi—the last name is Catalan, so he probably had Spanish roots—except that he was a member of a rather influential social club called the Boston Club. It's likely there that he befriended members of the krewe of Rex—or maybe he was a member himself. (The krewe of Rex is considered the first and most influential Mardi Gras krewe; see page 155.) By the early 1900s, the Ojen Cocktail had spread from the Boston Club to become Rex's pre-parade drink of choice. I'm not a member of Rex, but I am a sucker for tradition, so the Ojen Cocktail is my go-to drink before I ride during Mardi Gras each year.

Absinthe was banned in the U.S. in 1912 (see page 180), which must have struck quite a blow to its many fans in New Orleans. Luckily, a perfectly legal and similarly flavored substitute was already floating around the city, and Ojen found an even larger audience. By the time the original Morales family operation in Andalucía shut down, there were several competing Ojen brands, most notably one by Manuel Fernández of Jerez, who was the leading Ojen producer for decades.

Fernández cornered the Ojen market, but there was one problem: The market was tiny. The only people in the world who seemed to care about Ojen lived in New Orleans. Even in its native Spain, anise-flavored liqueurs had totally fallen out of fashion. By the late 1980s, Fernández decided to close down operations.

Thank god they gave us some notice. A local importer named Cedric Martin jumped to action. He called Fernández and made them an offer they couldn't refuse: Produce one final run of Ojen, and he'd buy the entire batch. Fernández made five hundred cases, more than six thousand bottles, and Martin bought them all.

According to Martin, the last bottle of the last run of Spanish Ojen was sold in 2009. We have some of those bottles at Cure, and we cherish them. But there is something so heartbreaking about drinking or selling the precious liquid. Each sip is a piece of history that, once consumed, is lost forever.

In 2016, the Sazerac Company decided they couldn't just let Ojen become some hyper-rarity that only wealthy collectors could access. Starting with a bottle of the Spanish original, they reverse-engineered their own Ojen, which they call Legendre Ojen. It is made in Kentucky from a grain distillate (rather than grapes, which was traditional in Spain), is available nationwide (although it might be harder to find the farther you are from New Orleans), and costs around $20.

Ojen isn't something I reach for every day, or even every month. But there are certain moments that demand it. I cannot imagine boarding a float and riding down St. Charles Avenue at Mardi Gras without first fortifying myself with an Ojen Cocktail at Arnaud's. So I am grateful to the Sazerac Company for keeping this odd little tradition alive.

OJEN COCKTAIL

For me, this is *the* drink of the Carnival season. It's so simple: basically an adult version of a Sno-ball, made pink and pretty by the addition of plenty of Peychaud's bitters. Although it isn't traditional, I sometimes add ½ ounce (15 ml) of orgeat (page 243), a nonalcoholic almond syrup flavored with orange flower water that is commonly used in tropical drinks. Orgeat was around in the 1800s and early 1900s, but I have no evidence of anyone using it in Ojen Cocktails—I simply find that it is a nice way to add richness and body to what can otherwise be a bracing drink. A bit of simple syrup could also work instead of the orgeat. (In either case, you should add even more Peychaud's, for balance.) Our official Cure recipe calls for 21 drops of bitters total, but when I'm making this for myself, I add even more.

2 ounces (60 ml) Ojen

14 drops Peychaud's bitters, plus 7 drops for garnish

Fill a chilled double-old fashioned glass with crushed ice. Pour the Ojen over the ice, add 14 drops of bitters, then stir or swizzle to agitate. Add more crushed ice to fill the glass, then stir or swizzle again. Add more crushed ice so it mounds over the rim of the glass, garnish with the remaining 7 drops of bitters, and serve.

Bittered Slings

CH. *2*

MANHATTANS

Stirred Drinks with Fortified Wine

CEASE AND DESIST
(PAGE 64)

To me, the Manhattan represents freedom. It's such a flexible template—2 ounces (60 ml) base spirit, 1 ounce (30 ml) fortified wine, and some bitters—you really can take it in whatever direction you want to go. Have you been eyeballing that bottle of Scotch? Make a Scotch Manhattan, also known as a Rob Roy. If you're feeling fancy, throw in a bit of Bénédictine to take it in the direction of a Bobby Burns. Got tequila? Grab some blanc vermouth and mole bitters, and you're on your way to a delicious, lightly spiced agave Manhattan.

Once you start exploring the category of fortified wines, the possibilities just explode. With one bottle of fortified wine, I can make a hundred different cocktails. The wine presents the flavor profile—it could be the spicy orange notes of the bitter Italian vermouth Punt e Mes or the nutty dried fruit of an oloroso sherry—and then I match different spirits and bitters to that. But why stop at one bottle of fortified wine? It's one of the most diverse categories out there, and there are so many amazing vermouths, quinquinas/chinottos, Madeiras, marsalas, ports, pineau des Charentes, rancio secs, and sherries worth exploring. I highly recommend going to the store and picking out a fortified wine you've never tried before, then, after tasting it on its own (slightly chilled and neat), try mixing up some Manhattans with it. Fortified wines have a relatively short fridge life of about two to four weeks, so you need to find creative ways to finish the bottle!

In the early days of the craft cocktail renaissance, when we had just opened Cure, we were all about Manhattan variations. It's just such a fun and easy template to riff on. A lot of people credit Enzo Errico, a New York bartender who worked at Milk & Honey, with kickstarting the Manhattan variation craze in 2003 when he created a Manhattan–Brooklyn hybrid called the Red Hook: 2 ounces (60 ml) rye, ½ ounce (15 ml) maraschino, ½ ounce (15 ml) Punt e Mes. It was the Manhattan's bitter, spicy cousin, and it inspired a bunch of so-called "neighborhood drinks": the Greenpoint, Carroll Gardens, Slope, and Bensonhurst.

At the time it all felt novel and exciting, but of course, what we were doing was nothing new. New Orleans bartenders throughout history were riffing on the Manhattan, just like modern bartenders were. Take a look at the classic New Orleans Vieux Carré (page 59), created at the Hotel Monteleone by Walter Bergeron in the 1930s. It's just a deconstructed Manhattan with a split rye–cognac base and a splash of cordial, served over ice. Another example is the Cocktail à la Louisiane, an equal-parts Manhattan with rye, Bénédictine, and Italian vermouth.

Since the golden age of mixology, bartenders have loved to play around with whatever new products come to market to see if they'd work in a Manhattan. In the late-nineteenth and early-twentieth centuries, those new products were imported Italian vermouths, absinthe, and cordials like Bénédictine. In the early 2000s, it was rye whiskey, Punt e Mes, Fernet-Branca, and Cynar. The ingredients changed, but the template stayed the same.

When I'm at home, the Manhattan is my go-to. I love that I can use whatever I have lying around. (It's a great way to use up that last ounce or two of any stray bottles, by the way.) If I'm feeling like something light and lower-ABV, I'll invert the template and mix two parts fortified wine to one part booze. If I only have an ounce of this and an ounce of that, I'll try splitting the base, using two complementary spirits like rye and brandy. What's great about the Manhattan is that it's choose-your-own-adventure, what people in the industry like to call a Mr. Potato Head cocktail. You can swap out the eyes or the nose or the hat (i.e., the modifier, base spirit, or bitters) to go wherever your creativity and taste take you. The result almost always ends up being satisfying.

MANHATTAN

Sometime around the 1870s or 1880s, bartenders came to the brilliant realization that if they stretched their pure-spirit cocktails with a bit of fortified wine, the resulting drink was a) delicious and b) lower proof, which meant bar patrons could drink more of them without falling out of their chairs. While New York City likes to take credit for its invention, the Manhattan was embraced from the start by the citizens of New Orleans (references to it were popping up in newspapers as early as 1885), which makes sense given our access to products like vermouth via our close trading relationships with Europe.

2 ounces (60 ml) Buffalo Trace bourbon

1 ounce (30 ml) Cinzano Rosso vermouth

14 drops Angostura bitters

Orange peel, for garnish

Combine all the ingredients except the garnish in a mixing glass filled with ice and stir to chill. Strain into a cocktail glass, garnish with the orange peel, and serve.

AMONG DREAMS

TURK DIETRICH

If you like Manhattans, I've just found your new favorite drink: Among Dreams is richer and smoother than any traditional Manhattan you'll taste. It's what we call an inverted Manhattan, meaning the vermouth—in this case, Carpano Antica, which was a favorite in the early days of the craft cocktail renaissance—is the base, or main ingredient, and the modifier, which is typically a fortified wine, is in this case rye whiskey. Turk balances the vanilla and orange notes of the Carpano with the herbaceousness of Chartreuse, and to kick up the proof a bit, he uses a spicy overproof rye. "I'm a sucker for aromatic bitters that have a Christmas-spice vibe, which you get from these Old-Fashioned bitters and the cinnamon from the tiki bitters," Turk says. Because of the higher proof of the modifiers (Chartreuse is 55% ABV; the bonded rye is 50%), this tastes like an even 50-50 Manhattan even though it's technically inverted.

2 ounces (60 ml) Carpano Antica Formula vermouth

½ ounce (15 ml) green Chartreuse

½ ounce (15 ml) Rittenhouse 100-proof rye

9 drops Bittermens 'Elemakule Tiki bitters

7 drops Fee Brothers Old Fashion bitters

Combine all the ingredients in a mixing glass filled with ice and stir until chilled. Strain into a chilled cocktail glass and serve.

CURE

MANHATTAN

VIEUX CARRÉ

Here's another New Orleans classic whose first book appearance was in 1937, in Stanley Clisby Arthur's *Famous New Orleans Drinks and How to Mix 'Em.* According to Arthur—and this is one of those rare instances where I think he got the story mostly right—the drink was invented by Walter Bergeron at the Hotel Monteleone, presumably in the years just following the repeal of Prohibition. Back then, the now-famous revolving Carousel Bar was just a twinkle in some marketing executive's eye, so guests would have enjoyed their Vieux Carrés gyration-free.

That said, we can't be entirely sure of when Bergeron first created the Vieux Carré. During Prohibition, he was the manager of a "cigar shop" that was raided in 1924. Bergeron was arrested for a gambling-related crime, but it's not hard to believe that he was slinging illegal hooch—Vieux Carrés, maybe?—in addition to cigars. Remember, New Orleans was called the "wettest city in America" during Prohibition (see page 62), so maybe Bergeron was lucky and his arresting officer was a Vieux Carré fan willing to turn a blind eye.

Our spec at Cure is pretty close to the classic formula, which blends American rye, Italian sweet vermouth, Caribbean bitters, French cognac, and the French liqueur Bénédictine. Some people like to say that the drink is a tribute to the diversity of the French Quarter (*vieux carré* means "old square") in those days when people of French, Italian, and Creole descent all lived side by side.

One last thing: If you studied French in school, you'll probably pronounce this "v-yoo car-ay." But in New Orleans we say "*voo* car-ay," because, well, it's New Orleans and we mispronounce everything.

¾ ounce (22.5 ml) Sazerac rye

¾ ounce (22.5 ml) Cinzano Rosso vermouth

¾ ounce (22.5 ml) Pierre Ferrand 1840 cognac

¼ ounce (7.5 ml) Bénédictine

14 drops Angostura bitters

14 drops Peychaud's bitters

Lemon peel, for garnish

Build the drink in a chilled double old-fashioned glass over 1 large ice cube or a few 1¼-inch (3-cm) pieces of ice. Garnish with the lemon peel and serve.

COCKTAIL À LA LOUISIANE

It doesn't take a cocktail genius to realize that the Cocktail à la Louisiane is just hedging its bet between a Sazerac and a Vieux Carré. For that reason, I always assumed that the drink was a sort of marketing ploy by the restaurant La Louisiane. They saw how well the Hotel Monteleone, which was just around the corner, was doing with their Vieux Carrés and decided that they needed a house cocktail, too. So they split the difference between the Vieux Carré and the other famous New Orleans drink, the Sazerac, and basically created the Cronut of cocktails. (They took two things that are outstanding on their own and combined them into something that is . . . edible, but does it really need to exist in the world? That said, many people love a Cronut and many love the Vieux Carré, so I encourage you to give the drink a try, even if it isn't quite on the same level as other New Orleans classics.)

Like so many of my well-reasoned cocktail theories, this one is damn hard to prove. The issue is, some people are convinced that the Cocktail à la Louisiane actually predates the Vieux Carré, since the restaurant La Louisiane opened in 1881, and in theory, the cocktail could have hit the menu before Prohibition.

One way to triangulate when the drink was created would be to figure out when Bénédictine, one of its key ingredients, first entered the New Orleans market. For this, I turned to my friend the cocktail scholar Wayne Curtis, who found a print ad for Bénédictine in a New Orleans newspaper in 1938. But, Curtis jokes, that only narrows down the time frame "plus or minus fifty years."

I don't know if we'll ever be able to state with certainty which came first, the Vieux Carré or the Cocktail à la Louisiane. In the grand spirit of Stanley Clisby Arthur, I'll share another wild theory that will be impossible for me to prove: What if both cocktails were invented at the same time, specifically for *Famous New Orleans Drinks*? I could totally see our man Arthur going to both the Monteleone and La Louisiane and telling them that if they whipped up something special for him, he'd include it in his book. Oh, and would they consider throwing in a free dinner in exchange for the coverage? Please and thank you.

4 spritzes Herbsaint

¾ ounce (22.5 ml) Sazerac rye

¾ ounce (22.5 ml) Bénédictine

¾ ounce (22.5 ml) Cinzano Rosso vermouth

21 drops Peychaud's bitters

Luxardo maraschino cherry, for garnish

Chill a cocktail glass, then spritz the Herbsaint from an atomizer into the interior of the glass. Combine all the ingredients except the garnish in a mixing glass filled with ice and stir to chill. Strain into the prepared glass, garnish with the cherry, and serve.

THE WETTEST CITY IN AMERICA: NEW ORLEANS DURING PROHIBITION

This should come as a surprise to no one, but the city of New Orleans wasn't really a willing participant during Prohibition. While the rest of the state of Louisiana, especially the Protestant parishes in the north, leaned dry, cosmopolitan New Orleans and the French, Catholic parishes of southwestern Louisiana were defiantly wet. Around here, no one was interested in the so-called Noble Experiment.

When the Louisiana state legislature first voted on whether to ratify the Eighteenth Amendment, the amendment failed in a tied 20-20 vote. But a short time later, despite the best efforts of the New Orleans delegation, some poor sap flipped. On August 6, 1918, the amendment passed 21 to 20. It was the closest vote of any state that approved the amendment.

At first, the citizens of New Orleans were in denial. They assumed that all the anti-booze, Anti-Saloon League fervor in the air was just a passing craze, and that it was only a matter of time before America came to its senses. There were somewhere around five thousand bars in the city at the time, and it seemed impossible that the government could actually find and close *all* of them.

That turned out to be somewhat true. When it opened its first headquarters in New Orleans, the Bureau of Prohibition appointed only ten enforcing agents to patrol the city. That number grew over time, but it never exceeded around thirty or forty. Keep in mind those agents were responsible for all of Orleans Parish and also expected to help across the state as needed. Local police were not particularly interested in assisting the short-staffed feds:

According to historian Joy Jackson in "Prohibition in New Orleans: The Unlikeliest Crusade," published in *Louisiana History*, in the last five years of Prohibition, state police made 322 booze-related arrests in Louisiana compared to federal agents' 6,022. Call it passive resistance, if you'd like.

From 1919 to 1933, it was never particularly hard to get a drink in New Orleans. As one story has it, the notorious Prohibition agent Izzy Einstein once came to New Orleans as part of an investigation to determine where in the country it was easiest to find illegal booze. New Orleans won in a cakewalk: It took him 35 seconds to score. The taxi driver who picked him up from the train station offered to sell him a bottle from under the seat.

In addition to taxis, you could also buy alcohol at fruit stands, pool halls, hotels, your neighbor's house (homebrewing "became an almost universal practice among Orleanians," according to Jackson), and of course, in the many bars and restaurants that refused to follow the rules. Fancier spots, like Delmonico's on St. Charles Ave., simply moved the booze consumption to private dining rooms. Some, like Commander's and Arnaud's, served it openly out of demitasse-style coffee cups, at least until they were raided. Many former saloons converted to "soft drink stands," which sold cheap homebrew to less affluent customers; others became speakeasies that catered to a more exclusive clientele. The most elite boozers of the South all congregated in New Orleans and from there set sail to Havana, often on steamships run by the United Fruit Company.

Why exactly was Prohibition so hard to enforce in New Orleans? If you're reading this book, you probably have a good idea: New Orleanians have always treated good food and good booze as their birthright. But there's also the fact that New Orleans was one of the biggest and most central alcohol distribution centers in the country, called the "liquor capital of America," or more poetically, the "wettest city in America." In the month before the Eighteenth Amendment went into effect, between December 1919 and January 1920, "99,991 gallons of whiskey and 1,332,380 gallons of alcohol sailed downriver from New Orleans docks headed mainly for South America," according to Jackson. Somehow, I don't think all of that product made it to its intended destination. Five years later, in 1925, two hundred out-of-town federal agents staged a series of raids that are considered the most significant in the history of Prohibition, dubbed the "clean-up of New Orleans." They seized ten thousand cases of liquor worth $1 million, an astonishing amount. But as one bootlegger is said to have quipped to the *Times-Picayune*, they "didn't get such an awful amount. I don't believe the price of liquor in New Orleans will go up much." New Orleans still had stockpiles of booze to spare.

Although New Orleans never really stopped drinking, we also never miss an opportunity to celebrate. So when Congress legalized beer in April 1933 (a first step toward total repeal, which happened on December 5, 1933), you better believe we partied with abandon. Local breweries prepared more than one million gallons of beer, which sped through the city streets on three hundred trucks (whose drivers got high on their own supply) to waiting bars, restaurants, and shops. More than nine hundred retail beer permits were issued in just a few days. Sirens, boat whistles, and car horns blared throughout the day to signal the good news: Finally, New Orleans could return to its natural state.

CEASE AND DESIST

MAKSYM PAZUNIAK

Here's another inverted Manhattan variation that I love because it's a showcase for so many of the ingredients we were obsessed with when we first opened Cure. First there's the bitter, orange-scented aperitivo Punt e Mes, which we were intrigued by because of the way it straddles the vermouth and amaro categories. Then there's the rye, an ingredient that is integral to many classic New Orleans cocktails but had completely fallen out of favor after Prohibition and was only just creeping back into the marketplace seventy-five years later. Last there's Fernet-Branca, an aggressively bitter liqueur that some people hate but that bartenders love to order to prove their bona fides. (Ordering a shot of Fernet used to be called the "bartender's handshake.")

As far as the name is concerned: Kirk and Maks wrote and self-published a cocktail book in 2009 called *Rogue Cocktails* that became a kind of underground hit among cocktail aficionados. Unfortunately, the Oregon-based craft brewery Rogue wasn't such a fan of the title. At least Maks got a good drink name out of their cease-and-desist letter.

2 ounces (60 ml) Punt e Mes

1 ounce (30 ml) Rittenhouse bottled-in-bond or Pikesville rye

1 barspoon Fernet-Branca

Orange peel, for garnish

Combine all the ingredients in a mixing glass filled with ice and stir until chilled. Strain into a chilled cocktail glass, garnish with the orange peel, and serve.

ESGANA CÃO

KIRK ESTOPINAL

Kirk is such a talented bartender, but maybe not the strongest drink-namer in Cure's history. The name of this drink translates to "dog strangler" in Portuguese. In Kirk's defense, Esgana Cão is a nickname for the Sercial grape from which the Madeira used in the recipe is made. Even so, I hope we never have any Portuguese-speaking guests in the bar when this one is on the menu.

The drink kind of straddles the line between a martini and a Manhattan: It's got great depth of flavor, but it's still very acidic and snappy. At Cure, we love to play around in the gray area between drink categories. Pagès is kind of hard to come by, but it has Chartreuse-like qualities. If you can't find it, Kirk suggests subbing in a mix of green and yellow Chartreuse (or just yellow in a pinch). If you're looking for another use for this Madeira, check out the Sea Dog (page 220).

4 spritzes Pagès Verveine Velay Extra liqueur

2 ounces (60 ml) Rare Wine Co. Charleston Sercial Madeira

1 ounce (30 ml) Germain Robin craft method brandy

14 drops Peychaud's bitters

2 orange peels, including 1 for garnish

Chill a cocktail glass, then spritz the Pagès from an atomizer into the interior of the glass. Combine the Madeira, brandy, and bitters in a mixing glass filled with ice and stir until chilled. Strain into the prepared cocktail glass, then express one of the orange peels and discard it. Mount the second orange peel and serve.

TRACK 61

COLIN BUGBEE

In his early days at Cure, Colin loved to take tiki flavors and try to make them fit in non-tiki, classic formats. "Track 61 is a hidden subway track below the Waldorf Astoria Hotel in New York City and is said to have been used to secretly transport presidents and other notable people," Colin explains. It's a fitting name for this rye Manhattan that sneaks in peppery green notes and tropical spices.

1 ounce (30 ml) Pikesville rye

¾ ounce (22.5 ml) Cardamaro vino amaro

¾ ounce (22.5 ml) Rucolino amaro

¼ ounce (7.5 ml) La Cigarrera manzanilla sherry

4 drops Bittermens 'Elemakule Tiki bitters

Orange peel

Combine all the ingredients in a mixing glass filled with ice and stir until chilled. Strain into a chilled cocktail glass, express and discard the orange peel, and serve.

WHISKY SINISTER

RYAN GANNON

This is essentially an equal-parts Manhattan, since there's an equal ratio of base spirit (in this case, Scotch) and fortified aromatized wine. For the wine component, Ryan decided to split between a classic cream sherry and a really interesting quina infused with wild cherry (which tastes a bit like cherry marzipan). You get nuttiness from the sherry, bitterness and dark fruit from the quina, and overall, a very pleasing brown, bitter, and stirred drink.

1½ ounces (45 ml) Sheep Dip 8-year pure malt Scotch

¾ ounce (22.5 ml) Maurin Quina Le Puy liqueur

¾ ounce (22.5 ml) Fernando de Castilla cream sherry

21 drops Angostura bitters

Combine all the ingredients in a mixing glass filled with ice and stir until chilled. Strain into a chilled cocktail glass and serve.

WHISKY SINISTER

THE HARDEST WALK

TURK DIETRICH

Here's another classic from the early days of Cure that is still so, so good. This recipe presents like an inverted (or vermouth-forward) Manhattan but drinks like an awesome rum Negroni. When I asked Turk how he came to this particular ingredient combination, he admitted that he and bartender Nick Jarrett used to pour equal parts of Punt e Mes and Plantation overproof rum and take it as a shot. A very intense, very high-proof shot. ("Yeah, we were psychopaths," Turk says.) But in a cocktail, the combo really works, especially with the fruity notes of Gran Classico and orange bitters balancing it all out. This is one of Turk's best.

2 ounces (60 ml) Punt e Mes

1 ounce (30 ml) Ron Hacienda Santa Ana overproof rum

⅛ ounce (3.75 ml) Tempus Fugit Gran Classico bitter

14 drops orange bitters

Orange peel, for garnish

Combine all the ingredients except the garnish in a mixing glass filled with ice and stir until chilled. Strain into a double old-fashioned glass filled with ice, garnish with the orange peel, and serve.

DARK IN THE CORNER

TURK DIETRICH

Turk will be the first to admit that he's a bit of a brooding guy. When he struck up a rapport with a couple of regulars who shared his dark sense of humor (and who liked to hide in the corner of the bar), one of them asked for a dealer's choice Manhattan riff and he decided to name this drink in their honor. "At this point, I was pretty sick of bourbon," he says. "Cognac is always a good substitute for a bourbon drinker, so I went with that." Adding a bit of Fernet was Turk's nod to another Cure classic, the Cease and Desist (page 64). We bartenders are always referencing each other's drinks in one way or another.

1½ ounces (45 ml) Pierre Ferrand 1840 cognac

1½ ounces (45 ml) Cocchi Storico vermouth di Torino

⅛ ounce (15 ml) Fernet-Branca

⅛ ounce (15 ml) Marie Brizard Apry apricot liqueur

7 drops Fee Brothers Old Fashion bitters

Orange peel, for garnish

Combine all the ingredients except the garnish in a mixing glass filled with ice and stir until chilled. Strain into a chilled cocktail glass, garnish with the orange peel, and serve.

Manhattans

THE VALLEY BELOW

GENEVIEVE MASHBURN

Genevieve's goal here was "to create a cocktail with flavors reminiscent of the famed New Orleans flaming coffee drink, the Café Brûlot." The Café Brûlot was purportedly created in the mid-1800s by Jules Alciatore, the son of the founder of Antoine's, an iconic French Quarter restaurant that is still up and running. Today, you can order a Brûlot at any number of old-school spots such as Antoine's, Arnaud's, Galatoire's, or Commander's. The recipe varies slightly from place to place, but the gist of it is the same: Cut an entire orange peel into a horse's neck–style garnish, stud it with cloves, and wrap it around the tines of a fork. Place brandy (which is often infused with cinnamon and citrus and sometimes augmented with kirsch or orange liqueur) in the bowl of a special apparatus called a brûlot set. Light the brandy on fire, then, using a ladle, spoon the flaming brandy over the studded orange peel. The citrus oils should ignite and provide a nice little fireworks display for your guests. Pour coffee into the bowl with the brandy to extinguish the flame, then sweeten the mixture with sugar before serving.

The Valley Below, by contrast, "involves considerably less pomp and pageantry," Genevieve tells me. She turned to our friends at HiVolt Coffee, a locally owned spot just off of Magazine Street in the Lower Garden District, and decided to use their cold brew concentrate (made with Counter Culture coffee) in a drink. She explains, "On paper, two amari may seem redundant—but the alpine, more herbal Braulio balances the sweeter, caramel flavor of Averna."

1 ounce (30 ml) El Dorado 12-year rum

½ ounce (15 ml) Averna amaro

½ ounce (15 ml) Braulio amaro

¾ ounce (22.5 ml) cold brew concentrate

7 drops Bittermens Xocolatl mole bitters

Lemon peel, for garnish

Combine all the ingredients except the garnish in a mixing glass filled with ice and stir until chilled. Strain into a chilled cocktail glass, garnish with the lemon peel, and serve.

TROUBLE & DESIRE

MICHAEL YUSKO

"My goal was to do something with the dusty bottle of Licor 43 nobody seemed to want anything to do with," Michael explains, referring to the citrus-and-vanilla-flecked liqueur that is popular in Spain but less well known here. "I figured it would be safe in this rum Manhattan variation." For the name, Michael turned to the 1992 Hal Hartley film *Simple Men*, in which a heartbroken and recently swindled character utters the iconic line, "There is no such thing as adventure. There is no such thing as romance. There's only trouble and desire."

2 ounces (60 ml) El Dorado 5-year rum

½ ounce (15 ml) Smith and Cross traditional Jamaican rum

½ ounce (15 ml) Licor 43 liqueur

¾ ounce (22.5 ml) Carpano Antica Formula vermouth

Orange peel, for garnish

Combine all the ingredients except the garnish in a mixing glass filled with ice and stir until chilled. Strain into a chilled double old-fashioned glass over 1¼-inch (3-cm) ice cubes, garnish with the orange peel, and serve.

Manhattans

THE NEW ORLEANS
COCKTAIL BUCKET LIST

Let's say it's your first time visiting New Orleans and you don't want to miss a single cocktail-related landmark. There are a lot of them, and the thing about cocktail bars is, it gets harder and harder to keep track of your checklist the deeper you go. So here's a handy cheat sheet of some of my favorite spots. Just make sure to pace yourself! You might not cover them all on your first trip, but that's the beauty of New Orleans: There's always an excuse to come back.

ARNAUD'S FRENCH 75 BAR. This will come as a surprise to no one, but Arnaud's does a mean **French 75**. That's what my wife always orders when we're there. But my preferred order is actually an **Ojen Cocktail** (page 51), especially if we're eating lunch.

GALATOIRE'S. Speaking of day drinking, Galatoire's is one of my favorite lunch spots in the city. There are few places I'd rather be at noon on a Friday than the crowded, buzzing, green-wallpapered dining room of Galatoire's, watching a server prepare my **Café Brûlot** tableside. There's nothing like a flaming, alcoholic coffee to really kick your day up to the next level.

SAZERAC BAR. Of course, you could order the namesake cocktail, but I'd actually go for their **Ramos Gin Fizz** (page 160).

HOTEL MONTELEONE. Go to the source and order a **Vieux Carré** (page 59) at its birthplace. Take a spin around the Carousel Bar while you're at it. (This is best if you have a small group that can all be seated together. Anyone left standing will quickly realize that the rest of their group has spun away. I can't tell you how many times during **Tales of the Cocktail** [see page 165] I got stuck standing next to seated friends and had to do this awkward sidestep dance to keep up.)

NAPOLEON HOUSE. The vibe at Napoleon House is *outstanding*. You're in this old French Quarter space; it's patinaed, with a bust of Napoleon and wood finishes everywhere; there's classical music playing. It can get jammed, but if you're lucky and catch them on a sleepier afternoon, order a roast beef po'boy and a **Pimm's Cup**, a cocktail with origins in Victorian England but that the Napoleon House adopted as a signature cocktail in the 1940s. Today, they make theirs with the decidedly un-Victorian addition of 7 Up, but it's still tasty. Sit back and enjoy one of the most quintessential New Orleans experiences there is.

TUJAGUE'S. Tujague's claims to be the second-oldest restaurant in New Orleans and home to the oldest continuously operating stand-up bar in the country. It's also famously the birthplace of the **Grasshopper**, a fluorescent concoction of crème de menthe, crème de cacao, and heavy cream. Definitely a polarizing drink, but my feeling is, when in Rome! It's not like I want to drink them all the time, but it's a pleasing drink, and a little bit is great. I had my first Grasshopper in Thailand when I was in my twenties. I remember thinking, "This is fucking awesome!" So I ordered another one. That second one, not as awesome. That's when I realized that some drinks are one-and-done.

BRENNAN'S. Milk, cream, vanilla, bourbon. It may sound intense, but trust me, the Brennan's **Milk Punch** is iconic and delicious. This is another instance where you should stop at one, though.

REVEL. There's nothing quite like sitting across the bar from a real-deal cocktail historian, which is why you have to visit my friends Chris and Laura McMillian's bar, Revel. Order from the menu and let Chris tell you a story about what you're drinking. He brings cocktail history to life better than anyone I know.

CHLOE HOTEL. Located in a nineteenth-century Uptown mansion, the bar at the Chloe Hotel is one of my favorite newer spots in the city. Try any of their originals.

JEWEL OF THE SOUTH. Chris Hannah is a legend and largely responsible for the popularity of brandy-based **French 75s** in New Orleans and beyond. Order a **75** from the maestro.

CANE & TABLE. Yes, I'm plugging my own spot. Folks used to say that New Orleans is the northernmost port of the Caribbean, and that's what we're trying to channel with our island-inspired menu at Cane & Table. If you're in the Quarter, swing by for a rum drink like the **Hurricane and Table** (page 104) and chef Alfredo Nogueira's coctel de camarones and empanadas.

PEYCHAUD'S. More unapologetic self-promotion! We opened Peychaud's in 2021 in the former home of Antoine Amédée Peychaud himself. As far as historic locales are concerned, you really can't do better. Order a **Sazerac** (page 27) in Peychaud's honor.

BAR TONIQUE. I actually put in the bar program at this spot on Rampart Street way back when. It's cozy and casual, and you can't go wrong ordering a classic like a **Moscow Mule**.

LATITUDE 29. I'm not a huge tiki guy, but I love Jeff "Beachbum" Berry and Annene Kaye-Berry, and their bar Latitude 29 is one of the best tiki bars in the country. My wife, Kea, actually did some legal work for them early on, and they thanked her with the **Kea Colada**, which is still on the menu! I'd probably stick to the tiki canon and order a **Mai Tai**.

TWELVE MILE LIMIT. Cole Newton has been doing the neighborhood craft cocktail bar thing for a long time, and he does it well. Head to Mid-City and order an original cocktail from their menu.

BARREL PROOF. Another great neighborhood spot in the Lower Garden District, specializing in whiskey—how about a nice **whiskey with a beer back**?

THE COLUMNS. Pick up the streetcar at Canal Street and ride it down beautiful, live oak–lined St. Charles Avenue. Hop off at Peniston Street and stroll over to the Columns Hotel, a white, Italianate mansion with one of the city's best verandahs for cocktails and people-watching.

PREVIOUS PAGE
Napoleon House
OPPOSITE, TOP TO BOTTOM
Tujague's, Galatoire's
NEXT SPREAD
Carousel Bar at the Hotel Monteleone

MARTINIS

Clear, Boozy, and Stirred Drinks

AMPELOS
(PAGE 82)

I have lots of opinions about lots of cocktails, but when it comes to the martini, I defer to my guests. More so than any other drink, the martini is about personal choice. Maybe you like yours wet; maybe you like it dry; maybe you like it with gin, or with vodka. My wife prefers a dirty martini with tons of brine, and who am I to judge? What draws so many people to the martini is that you can put your own personal stamp on it. As a proprietor and host, I would never want to take that away from you.

In the early days of Cure, we were a bit more dogmatic—some might even say inflexible. But back then, we were really trying to steer our guests away from their standard orders of a Jack and Coke or Belvedere and soda. People had been conditioned to order cocktails based on *brand*, not what they wanted to drink. We used to say that the "automatic order" was our enemy. So we didn't carry most mainstream brands, and we only ever had one or two vodkas on the backbar. If you came in and ordered a martini, we tended to serve you something close to the recipe on page 80.

In our defense, we were trying to right all the wrongs the martini had suffered over the years. There was a moment in the 1980s or 1990s when it became a nine-ounce (265 ml) drink that was basically straight vodka, designed to fuck you up. And then the suffix -*tini* got attached to all these cocktails that it shouldn't have been attached to. So I feel like you really can't blame craft cocktail bartenders for trying to push drinkers toward a more restrained, "pure" version of the drink in the 2000s and 2010s. We wanted to show people how incredible vermouth can be if it's stored and served properly. (So many people who think they don't like vermouth-heavy "wet" martinis have just been drinking spoiled vermouth.)

In those first years of Cure, I think some people genuinely hated us. But eventually people moved away from their automatic orders and started exploring new categories of drink. Paradoxically, that's exactly when we felt like we could loosen up a bit about our martinis. We didn't have to take such a hard line, because our guests were more curious and attuned to their tastes rather than to a liquor commercial they had seen on TV.

The cocktails in this chapter run the gamut from traditional to avant-garde. They're all delicious and proof that there's more than one way to enjoy a martini.

DAUPHINE'S MARTINI

My go-to martini order is actually an inverted martini. I'm kind of a lightweight (and not trying to win any races to the bottom of the bottle), so a standard martini has the tendency to knock me on my ass.

At our Washington, D.C., restaurant, Dauphine's, we serve what I like to think of as an inverted-plus martini: two parts vermouth, one part gin, but with a navy-strength gin to give it a bit more oomph. We spritz the glass with anise to give it that extra New Orleansy touch. That may seem sacrilegious to martini purists, but in fact, martinis were often "improved" with absinthe in the early 1900s, so it's not such a historical anomaly.

4 spritzes Herbsaint

1 ounce (30 ml) Plymouth navy-strength gin

1 ounce (30 ml) La Quintinye Extra Dry Royal vermouth

1 ounce (30 ml) Poli Gran Bassano bianco vermouth

7 drops Bittercube orange bitters

Lemon peel, for garnish

Chill a cocktail glass, then spritz the Herbsaint from an atomizer into the interior of the glass. Combine the gin, vermouth, and bitters in a mixing glass filled with ice and stir to chill. Strain into the prepared cocktail glass, garnish with the lemon peel, and serve.

CURE MARTINI

For years, our house martini was the 50-50 on page 83. However, we recently switched to a slightly drier 2:1 martini. Using fresh vermouth remains essential.

2 ounces (60 ml) London dry gin

1 ounce (30 ml) Noilly Prat Original dry vermouth

3 drops Regans' orange bitters

Lemon peel or olives skewered on a cocktail pick, for garnish

Combine the gin, vermouth, and bitters in a mixing glass filled with ice and stir to chill. Strain into a chilled cocktail glass, garnish with the lemon peel or olives, and serve.

DAUPHINE'S MARTINI

AMPELOS

RYAN GANNON

"I decided that I wanted to do a flash-pickle—something super quick, with no brining salts or anything like that—that we could have behind the bar," Ryan said. "Weirdly enough, for this drink I kind of worked backward from the garnish." Mirliton is the local Louisiana name for the green, pear-shaped squash known elsewhere as chayote; it's a classic summer ingredient down here. "In Greek mythology, all wines come from Ampelos's desiccated body. I thought that was a cool, vivid name for a drink made only with grape products" (pisco, vermouth, sherry, and Sainte Louise brandy are all grape-based spirits). (See photo on page 78.)

¾ ounce (22.5 ml) Caravedo puro
    quebranta pisco

¾ ounce (22.5 ml) La Quintinye royal
    blanc vermouth

¾ ounce (22.5 ml) Valdespino amontillado
    sherry

¾ ounce (22.5 ml) Sainte Louise brandy

1 teaspoon (5 ml) mirliton pickle juice (see
    Pickled Mirliton recipe at right)

5 drops Bittermens Boston Bittahs

Slice of Pickled Mirliton (recipe follows),
    skewered on a cocktail pick, for garnish

Combine all the ingredients except the garnish in a mixing glass filled with ice and stir until chilled. Strain into a chilled cocktail glass and garnish with the pickled mirliton.

Pickled Mirliton

MAKES 1 PINT (480 ML)

1 mirliton (chayote), about 8 ounces (225 g)

¾ cup (180 ml) white vinegar

¾ cup (180 ml) white sugar

1 tablespoon kosher salt

Cut the mirliton in half and scrape away the seeds. Cut the flesh into ⅛-inch-wide (3-mm) French fry shapes and soak in ice water while you prepare the brine.

In a small saucepan, combine the vinegar, sugar, salt, and 1 cup (240 ml) water and bring to a boil over high heat. At the first crack of a boil, remove the pan from the heat. Place the mirliton in a heatproof nonreactive pint-size (480-ml) container and pour the brine over the top. Make sure the mirliton is fully submerged (add water to top if necessary). Refrigerate for at least 1 hour before using or up to 1 week.

CURE

50-50 MARTINI

This is what we call a 50-50 or "fitty-fitty" martini in the biz. That's because we use equal parts gin and vermouth to create a very wet martini. If you think you don't like wet martinis, please just give this a try. So long as your vermouth is fresh, I guarantee it will change your mind.

1½ ounces (45 ml) London dry gin

1½ ounces (45 ml) Noilly Prat Original dry vermouth

7 drops Regans' orange bitters

Lemon peel, for garnish

Combine the gin, vermouth, and bitters in a mixing glass filled with ice and stir to chill. Strain into a chilled cocktail glass, garnish with the lemon peel, and serve.

5-TO-1 MARTINI

When people ask for a dry martini, this is what we serve them: just a whisper of vermouth, heavy on the gin, with a lemon peel or high-quality olives, depending on the guest's preference.

2½ ounces (75 ml) Bombay dry gin

½ ounce (15 ml) Noilly Prat Original dry vermouth

3 drops Regans' orange bitters

Lemon peel or olives skewered on a cocktail pick, for garnish

Combine the gin, vermouth, and bitters in a mixing glass filled with ice and stir to chill. Strain into a chilled cocktail glass, garnish with the lemon peel or olives, and serve.

Martinis

PERSONALITY CRISIS

NICHOLAS JARRETT

This bitter, fruity, and vegetal inverted martini takes advantage of the brilliant pairing of strawberry and Alta Verde amaro. Alta Verde is an assertive bitter liqueur that's in a category called *gentianes* (named for the main ingredient, gentian root) made in Alto Adige, in Northern Italy. It is famously hard to work with. The primary tasting note is *assenzio,* an Alpine wormwood variety that some people describe as tasting like a summer forest. Given how much early New Orleanians loved wormwood-flavored absinthes, I like to imagine this drink might have been a hit, even back in the day. The Alta Verde marries beautifully with strawberry, as does tequila, so Nick had the smart idea of using strawberry as the unifying flavor across the drink.

1 strawberry, hulled

¼ ounce (7.5 ml) Alta Verde amaro

2 ounces (60 ml) Cocchi Americano Rosa Aperitivo vermouth

1 ounce (30 ml) Siembra Valles blanco tequila

Combine the strawberry and amaro in a mixing glass and muddle. Add the vermouth and tequila, fill the mixing glass with ice, then stir until chilled. Fine-strain into a double old-fashioned glass over 1 large ice cube and serve.

EYEDAZZLER

NICHOLAS JARRETT

Nick describes this drink as "a through-the-looking-glass take on a reverse martini, combining our go-to French dry vermouths against a subtle blend of fine Pennsylvanian potato vodka, French cognac, and just a whiff of London dry gin." What I love about this drink is the way Nick flips the dry martini totally on its head. Plenty of people ask for a super-dry gin martini with no more than a hint of vermouth. Here, Nick starts with a base of vermouth, augments it with vodka, and then just spritzes the surface of the drink with gin so you get those juniper notes on the nose.

1 ounce (30 ml) Boyd and Blair potato vodka

1 ounce (30 ml) Dolin dry vermouth

1 ounce (30 ml) Noilly Prat Original dry vermouth

½ ounce (15 ml) Augier cognac

7 drops Bittermens orange cream citrate

2 drops Saline Solution (page 243)

1 spritz Tanqueray gin

Lemon peel, for garnish

Combine all the ingredients except the gin and the garnish in a mixing glass filled with ice and stir until chilled. Strain into a chilled cocktail glass, then spritz the gin over the surface of the drink with an atomizer. Garnish with the lemon peel and serve.

Martinis

IAN NEVILLE on the Best New Orleans Music Venues

Ian Neville is a New Orleans native and guitarist in the funk band Dumpstaphunk. He is also the son of Art "Poppa Funk" Neville of the Neville Brothers—and a big fan of cocktails (the two of us met when I worked at a neighborhood spot called the Delachaise).

Turns out, we've been running in the same circles for a while. When interviewing him for this book, I learned that he and I crossed paths in 1995, when I was a bouncer at a place called the Rendon Inn. I use the term "bouncer" loosely; I was eighteen and not exactly imposing. Mostly my job was to attract other eighteen-year-olds to come drink there (the drinking age was still eighteen in Louisiana at the time). I definitely wasn't doing a good job carding, because apparently thirteen-year-old Ian made it into a Marilyn Manson show in the Hangar. He remembers climbing up and sitting on a ledge so his feet were resting on the push bar of one of the exits (fire hazard!). I remember a bonfire in the middle of the Hangar and naked people jumping through and spraying each other with chocolate sauce (also a fire hazard).

The Rendon Inn isn't a music venue anymore, but I was able to chat with him about his favorite spots in New Orleans to see local musicians and enjoy a drink or two.

Where do you like to go to have a drink and listen to music?

There are plenty of places to see good music and plenty of places to get some solid beverages. Do those line up all the time? Unfortunately, not often. But **d.b.a** (618 Frenchmen St.) gets close! They are in the middle of the Venn diagram of good venues with good drink selections—especially whiskeys and mezcals.

Speaking of mezcal, my little sister played at **Banks Street Bar** (4401 Banks St.). It's the strangest bar to have such a dope selection of mezcal—I walked in and was like, "How did that Bozal get here?"

My home court is **Tipitina's** (501 Napoleon Ave.). I could say it's world-renowned and all that, but the truth is I've been going there since I was literally one year old. Tipitina's just has a kind of history and energy that's hard to feel anywhere else.

Maple Leaf (8316 Oak St.) is another super-local New Orleans hang. These days you don't stick to the bathroom floor, and they cleaned up a lot of the weird New Orleans-ness, but it's still a different, special kind of place.

There isn't really a hip, underground spot for me in New Orleans right now—it used to be **Mimi's** [Mimi's in the Marigny, which at the time of this writing is closed, but is rumored to possibly reopen]. But now I tell people to go find **DJ Soul Sister** [a fantastic DJ specializing in rare groove; visit djsoulsister.com]. She's a moving target for cool underground things.

What should an out-of-towner expect at these venues?

Think of it like you're going to a house party show. It's not formal; there won't be a metal detector or valet parking. You're just going with a group to a very familiar place to hang out. Don't expect overly crafted drink options. Don't kill the vibe or try to get fancy with people; just listen to music and have some fun!

HOLY GHOSTED

COLIN BUGBEE

There was a bottle of Belle de Brillet pear liqueur that had been sitting on our backbar for far too long. Whenever a bottle like that starts collecting dust, we have to ask ourselves why. Does it suck? In the case of the Belle de Brillet, no! It was and remains a great product. It had simply lost our attention for a while. That happens with products; their popularity ebbs and flows. Colin decided that the best way to bring the Belle de Brillet back was in this delicious martini variation, which has pear, a lovely chamomile note from the Noilly Prat, and a bit of salinity from the pistachio tincture. What can I say? It's a really pretty little cocktail.

1¼ ounces (37.5 ml) Noilly Prat Original dry vermouth

1 ounce (30 ml) Mattei Cap Corse Blanc quinquina

¾ ounce (22.5 ml) Belle de Brillet pear liqueur

8 drops Salted Pistachio Tincture (recipe follows)

Combine all the ingredients in a mixing glass filled with ice and stir until chilled. Strain into a chilled cocktail glass and serve.

Salted Pistachio Tincture

MAKES ½ CUP (120 ML)

½ cup (65 g) salted shelled pistachios

½ cup (120 ml) vodka, or as needed

In a small nonreactive container, combine the pistachios and enough vodka to barely cover the pistachios. Cover the container and let sit at room temperature for 48 hours. Strain the mixture and store the vodka in a nonreactive container for up to 6 months.

PROMISES, PROMISES

SUMMER ROMANCE

MATT LOFINK

"I like to take old drinks that nerdy bartenders and pretentious people scoff at and make them good," Matt tells me. For the Summer Romance, Matt started with one of the most scoffed-at drinks around, the appletini. "I didn't want to be in-your-face about it. I wanted it to be so subtle that people didn't realize it was an appletini; they'd just say, 'Oh, this martini has some nice apple notes to it.'" To get there, Matt embraced the fresh, green-apple notes of Montanaro vermouth and paired it with Cloosterbitter, an herbaceous liqueur that is probably closest to green Chartreuse but a bit lighter, sweeter, and lower proof. I didn't know that I needed an apple-tini in my life until I sipped this drink.

1½ ounces (45 ml) Plymouth gin

½ ounce (15 ml) Boomsma Cloosterbitter liqueur

½ ounce (15 ml) Montanaro bianco vermouth

7 drops Bar Keep apple bitters

Lemon peel, for garnish

Combine all the ingredients except the garnish in a mixing glass filled with ice and stir to chill. Stir a bit longer than you might normally—this drink benefits from the extra dilution. Strain into a chilled double old-fashioned glass filled with ice, garnish with the lemon peel, and serve.

PROMISES, PROMISES

NICHOLAS JARRETT

Nick was inspired by legendary New York bartender Julie Reiner's Gin Blossom (a martini augmented by a measure of apricot eau-de-vie) and Phil Ward's Elder Fashioned (a bourbon Old-Fashioned with elderflower liqueur) when he created this martini on the rocks. It's citrusy, aromatic, and refreshing.

1½ ounces (45 ml) Plymouth gin

¾ ounce (22.5 ml) Cocchi Americano Bianco Aperitivo vermouth

¼ ounce (7.5 ml) Giffard crème de pamplemousse liqueur

7 drops Bittermens hopped grapefruit bitters

Orange peel, for garnish

Combine all the ingredients except the garnish in a mixing glass filled with ice and stir until chilled. Strain into a double old-fashioned glass filled with ice, garnish with the orange peel, and serve.

Martinis

TWO-WAY MIRROR

TURK DIETRICH

Here's an awesome inverted martini with a home-made sage syrup. It's so simple and so subtle, but so delicious. "When I made this drink, that was the moment when Kirk said, 'OK, you've basically figured out cocktails now,'" Turk tells me. Given Kirk's high standards, that should tell you what you need to know.

2 ounces (60 ml) Dolin dry vermouth

½ ounce (15 ml) Sipsmith navy-strength gin

½ ounce (15 ml) Sage Syrup (recipe follows)

7 drops Bitter Truth celery bitters

7 drops Peychaud's bitters

Sage leaf, for garnish

Combine all the ingredients except the garnish in a mixing glass filled with ice and stir until chilled. Strain into a double old-fashioned glass filled with ice, garnish with the sage leaf, and serve.

Sage Syrup

MAKES ABOUT 1 CUP (240 ML)

10 fresh sage leaves

1 cup (200 g) sugar

Muddle the sage leaves in the tin of a cocktail shaker, then pour 1 cup (240 ml) very hot water over the top. Let sit for 8 minutes, until the water is infused with the sage. Strain out the sage leaves, add the sugar, and stir until dissolved. Store airtight in the fridge for up to 2 weeks.

CHERI CHERI

KIRK ESTOPINAL

Here's another of Kirk's dessert-influenced drinks and one of his personal faves. "En rama" is an unfiltered style of sherry, and here it contributes a rich nuttiness, which is complemented by the almondy orgeat, warm holiday spices from the bitters, and a subtle banana note from the arrack. Kirk is big into music, and this recipe gets its name from one of Bruce Springsteen's favorite songs, "Cheree," by the band Suicide.

1½ ounces (45 ml) La Gitana "en rama" sherry

¾ ounce (22.5 ml) Van Oosten Batavia arrack

¼ ounce (7.5 ml) Orgeat (page 243)

4 drops Fee Brothers Old Fashion bitters

Freshly ground nutmeg, for garnish

Combine all the ingredients except the garnish in a mixing glass filled with ice and stir until chilled. Strain into a chilled cocktail glass, garnish with three Microplane scrapes of fresh nutmeg, and serve.

CLASSIC DIVE BARS

Back in the old days, my dive bar order was a tequila on the rocks. Now that I'm older and wiser, I have two go-to orders, both pretty hard to mess up: a blended Scotch like Dewar's with soda and a lemon, or a bottle of Bud and a shot of Hennessy, Courvoisier, or whatever cognac they have. Or maybe a rye, if they have something I like.

Far be it from me to tell you what to order at a dive bar, though. It's all about personal expression. But no matter what you decide to drink, don't miss any of these classic spots.

THE SAINT. When I used to go to the Saint, which is a block off Magazine Street in a kind of strange location between the Garden and Lower Garden districts, it was very mellow—just a fun dive bar that stayed open late. Since then, it has changed ownership, and the new guys, one of whom is my friend Benji, really poured gas on it. So now the Saint has totally blown up, and it is *the* late-night dive bar in New Orleans. The photo booth there will provide you with a souvenir of your evening, whether you want to remember it or not. The Saint will always hold a special place in my heart, though, because it's where I got back together with my wife, Kea.

SNAKE AND JAKE'S CHRISTMAS LOUNGE. What's the story with the year-round Christmas bar at East Carrollton, you ask? Well, what *isn't* the story? I've been going to Snake and Jake's for years, even back when they hosted Naked Night. (If you came in naked, you drank for free. This is no longer done, for obvious reasons.) Although I never rolled up au naturel, I've had some very good, and very strange, times there. I'm always so happy when I'm inside Snake and Jake's; less so when I walk out and realize the sun is already peeking up over the horizon. Then I have to start questioning my life choices.

BROTHERS III. A classic on Magazine Street. This is where we used to go for a drink after work back in the days when I used to go out drinking after work. It's not too far from Cure, just a mile or so down Napoleon.

CHART ROOM. I used to hit up this French Quarter spot when I was nineteen and working at Bacco as a host. They had ice chests full of frozen domestic beers—heaven. In those days they had ten-ounce (300 ml) ponies; they've since switched to standard twelve-ouncers (360 ml), which I am really upset about. When I was a kid and trying to impress the older guys I worked with, we'd order shots of Chartreuse and light them on fire. Until one day, I raised up my hand to take the shot, still holding the just-used lighter, and burned my face. You will not be surprised to learn I have moved on from flaming shots.

ROBERT'S BAR. If you're shocked that I was out drinking at bars when I was nineteen, well, it's New Orleans. Robert's is where I used to go when I was *fifteen*. My parents always knew that I was getting up to high-school mischief (again, it's New Orleans), but they had to draw the line when I came home one night, arms full of Jägermeister gear and tchotchkes, after spending too much time with the Jägerettes.

KINGPIN. Owned by my pals Steve and Ben (who also own Midway Pizza, right across from Cure), Kingpin was kind of a clubhouse for my friends and I for many years. Nothing fancy; they just run a great shop.

LE BON TEMPS ROULE. Here's where you go to shoot pool on Magazine Street, late-late night. There used to be a guy, maybe in his fifties, who'd roll up in his Mercedes at 4 A.M., clearly in no state to be driving, then he'd pull out his own pool stick and head to the tables. And everyone would kind of roll their eyes, but even if he was too far gone to have a conversation, he could still shoot some pool. There are always characters at Le Bon Temps Roule. Come earlier than 4 A.M. and you can catch some live music.

ST. JOES'S BAR. I know calling this a dive bar is a stretch (it's a nice place!), but St. Joe's has all the features you'd want from a nice dive: a long bar, a pool table, and a place to sit outside. It's also been around for ages, and is an Uptown institution. So if you're in the neighborhood, swing through and have a beer seated under one of the crosses hung from the ceiling.

THE ERIN ROSE. This tiny French Quarter bar is famous for its frozen Irish Coffee. It's a great place to have your first drink upon landing in New Orleans. Grab a shot or a frozen Irish Coffee, sit down, and just take it all in. If you get hungry, grab a sandwich at Killer Poboys in the back.

MS. MAE'S. In my day, we used to call this "The Club," and I'm sure people still call it "The Club Ms. Mae's." I remember when I was a kid, whenever we used to stand in line for Casamento's (a classic restaurant on the same block), I'd just stare at the neon Ms. Mae's sign and wonder, *What goes on in there?* The answer, I've since learned, is fun times. The drinks are cheap, it's open 24 hours, and it's on one of the strongest corners in Uptown. Highly recommend.

PAL'S LOUNGE. My brother used to live next door to Pal's. *Truly* next door, as in, they shared a wall. I would categorize this as one of the classier dives. They often have great food pop-ups, so check their calendar.

PREVIOUS PAGE

Snake and Jake's Christmas Lounge

OPPOSITE

Pal's Lounge

BRANDY CRUSTA
(PAGE 110)

CH. *4*

SOURS

Bright, Refreshing Drinks with Citrus

There's a reason this is the longest chapter in the book. Everybody loves a sour. It's the most refreshing cocktail template there is and is especially popular down here in New Orleans, where the climate necessitates a lot of outdoor drinking. Unless it's winter, you don't really sit outside drinking a Sazerac. You want something bright, acidic, and thirst-quenching, like a daiquiri or margarita. That's why we always have plenty of sours on our menu at Cure and why they're always top sellers.

One might assume that contemporary drinkers' love of sours grew out of the "juicy martini" culture of the 1990s and early 2000s. After all, people developed a taste for fruity and acidic drinks like the appletini—even if those flavors were synthetic. But at least here in New Orleans, sour culture has much deeper roots.

I've talked a lot about the French and Spanish colonial influence on New Orleans's early cocktail culture. But there's another group that often gets left out of the conversation, who I would argue had a longer-lasting and farther-reaching impact—not only on New Orleans but also throughout the United States. They are the Sicilian merchants who came to New Orleans in the 1830s and brought along with them their most prized regional product: lemons.

People talk about chain migration—the process by which migrants from one town or region follow each other to settle in a new place. It's how nineteenth-century New Orleans ended up with a neighborhood called Little Palermo in the French Quarter. The main driver of that chain migration, both in Louisiana and in places with large Sicilian populations like New York and San Francisco, was the lemon trade.

Before I get too far ahead of myself, it's worth mentioning some of the other, noncitrus contributions Sicilian immigrants made to New Orleans food culture. To name them all would take more pages than I have, so I'll list just a few: the muffuletta, a signature New Orleans sandwich with salami, provolone, and olive tapenade; Progresso-brand soups, founded in New Orleans in 1925; Commander's Palace, opened by Emile Commander, son of Pietro Camarda (technically from Ustica a small island off the Sicilian coast); the Hotel Monteleone, now home to the famous revolving Carousel Bar, first opened by a Sicilian shoemaker; and the Dole Fruit Company, originally the Vaccaro brothers' Standard Fruit Company, an import business whose legacy of violent oppression and exploitation in Latin America is too dark to get into here. (Look up the history of so-called "banana republics" if you want to learn more.)

But back to those lemons. The first lemon cargoes arrived in New Orleans from Palermo in the 1830s. The lemon was ripe (sorry, I couldn't resist) for international stardom because it could be picked green and, if stored properly, would improve over the course of a long sea voyage. Lemons were used for preservation and essential to the canning industry until at least World War I. They were also prized for their medicinal properties. Even though people didn't quite understand the benefits of vitamin C, they knew that lemons were good for their health. And of course, lemons were incredibly popular for cooking, for the obvious reason that they taste delicious. According to historian Justin Nystrom, by 1884, lemons were New Orleans's third most valuable imported commodity, behind only coffee and sugar.

When did Sicilian-imported lemons start finding their way into cocktails? We know that Joseph Santini was squeezing their juice and artfully coiling their peels into his Brandy Crustas (page 110) at the Hotel St. Louis in the 1850s. After that, the lemon-juice floodgates opened, and gin sours, rum sours, brandy sours, and eventually whiskey sours became a nationwide phenomenon.

In this chapter, you'll find a few classics with a connection to New Orleans—the Brandy Crusta, the Hurricane, and a blended daiquiri, to name a few. But most of the recipes here are Cure originals, where we start from the basic template of boozy-sour-sweet and riff from there. What ties all these drinks together is 1) they're damn refreshing, and 2) they would be nothing without that backbone of beautiful citrus that made its way to our town nearly two hundred years ago.

HURRICANE AND TABLE

KIRK ESTOPINAL

The Hurricane is one of those cocktails that gets lumped together with the Hand Grenade and frozen daiquiri as a symbol of Bourbon Street debauchery. Here's the difference, though: I find the Hand Grenade, a sickly sweet melon concoction, pretty irredeemable. But there's a time and a place for a frozen daiquiri (see page 142), and I really like a well-made Hurricane.

The Hurricane was invented at Pat O'Brien's, a French Quarter institution that has officially been around since 1933. (Although ol' Pat was almost certainly running a speakeasy during Prohibition: Someone once asked me to check out the old speakeasy's location on Royal Street and St. Peter for a potential new bar.) Today, it's a bit of a tourist trap, but if you're in the market for dueling pianos and a flaming, neon-lit fountain, it's worth a visit.

The Hurricane is still Pat O'Brien's signature drink. Legend has it that it was created in the 1940s when domestic spirits like whiskey were scarce but Caribbean rum was plentiful, so distributors essentially told their accounts that if they wanted the good stuff like bourbon, they had to buy large quantities of rum, too. The Hurricane was created as a way to move the cases of rum that were collecting dust.

These days you can buy Pat O'Brien's premade Hurricane mix in powdered or liquid form. I won't speculate as to what they use to prepare their drinks at the restaurant, but I do know this: I don't want to drink a cocktail that comes from a packet, like Kool-Aid.

Our resident cocktail genius, Kirk, decided one day to reverse-engineer a Hurricane using premium rum and natural ingredients. It's incredible and does really well at Cane & Table. You have two options when you make it at home: You can make his tropical Hurricane Syrup from scratch using passion fruit puree and guava jelly, or you can buy a high-quality *fassionola,* the tropical fruity syrup that is essential in this drink (and some tiki drinks), from a reputable source like Cocktail & Sons. The only dehydrated ingredient I'm allowing here is the garnish, but you can also swap in a fresh orange wheel.

1½ ounces (45 ml) Don Q "Cristal" blanco rum

½ ounce (15 ml) Appleton 12-year rum

¾ ounce (22.5 ml) Cocktail & Son's fassionola, or Hurricane Syrup (recipe on page 106)

¾ ounce (22.5 ml) fresh lime juice

Dehydrated orange wheel, for garnish

Cocktail umbrella, for garnish

Combine all the ingredients except the garnishes in a shaker filled with ice. Quick-shake, then double-strain into a hurricane glass filled with crushed ice. Garnish with the orange wheel, umbrella, and a straw, and serve.

Hurricane Syrup

MAKES ABOUT 1 CUP (240 ML)

....

½ cup (120 ml) passion fruit puree

1 cup (200 g) white sugar

1 tablespoon (15 ml) pomegranate molasses

1 tablespoon (15 ml) Goya guava jelly, cut into small pieces

¼ ounce (7 g) dried hibiscus flowers

In a small saucepan, combine the passion fruit puree and 1 cup (240 ml) water and heat over medium heat until gently steaming. Add the sugar and pomegranate molasses and stir until dissolved. Add the guava jelly and stir until dissolved. Remove the saucepan from the heat and stir in the hibiscus flowers. Let cool to room temperature, strain out the hibiscus flowers, and decant into a nonreactive container. Store airtight in the refrigerator for up to 1 month.

The courtyard at Pat O'Brien's

THE ST. CHARLES: THE GRAND HOTEL OF NEW ORLEANS'S GRAND PAST

I think a lot of people forget that New Orleans was, for much of our nation's early history, one of the largest and most significant cities in America. As I mentioned, it was the country's third most populous city and a major economic center that attracted visitors from all over the world.

To me, one of the greatest embodiments of New Orleans's global importance was the St. Charles Hotel, also called the Exchange Hotel, a massive, multistory building that was a fixture of the city's downtown area for 137 years.

When its owners first welcomed guests to 201 St. Charles Avenue in 1837, their ambition was to operate the finest luxury hotel in the country, if not the world. Most people agree that it was definitely up there, on par with places like Astor House in New York City. The original building (which burned and was rebuilt in the 1850s) was an imposing five stories tall, with giant Corinthian columns, marble staircases, and a one-hundred-eighty-foot domed cupola.

The St. Charles was basically a gravity well that sucked other businesses into its orbit. Henry Ramos's saloons the Imperial Cabinet and the Stag were just two of the many drinking establishments that opened in its shadow. According to Southern culinary historian Robert Moss in *Southern Spirits*, hotel guests would send waiters to the Imperial Cabinet "bearing silver trays to place orders for a half dozen fizzes at a time in exchange for generous tips."

Guests of the hotel included businessmen and politicians, cotton and sugar planters, and well-heeled tourists from as far as Stockholm and Buenos Aires. More interesting to me, though, were the comings and goings into the octagonal basement bar, which before it burned down featured twenty-foot ceilings and was encircled by a commanding array of Ionic columns. Presumably, it is the birthplace of the hotel's signature libation, the St. Charles Punch. (For anyone keeping score, the only notable cocktail the rival St. Louis Hotel can lay claim to is the Brandy Crusta, page 110, which was created by Joseph Santini either there or at Jewel of the South. For my money, the St. Charles Punch is an infinitely better drink.)

The first St. Charles Hotel burned in 1851. It was rebuilt two years later, then burned again in 1894 and once again, was rebuilt two years later. The final nail in the coffin came in 1974, when it was demolished and replaced by a fifty-two-story skyscraper, the Place St. Charles.

As a beverage professional obsessed with New Orleans drinking history, I've always had a certain fascination with the St. Charles Hotel, an epic establishment where everyone from American presidents to British royals wined and dined.

So my mind was kind of blown when one day, I realized that it was still around when my dad was a young man in New Orleans. By then, although it still took up an entire block, its shine had started to fade. In the 1970s, the hotel was more likely to host a business convention than international royalty. Once the St. Charles was gone, there was never a comparably luxurious hotel that took its place. New York had the Astor and still has the Plaza; Paris has the Ritz; London, the Savoy—amazing hotels that were keystones of their city. New Orleans was once that kind of city, and the St. Charles was our crown jewel. So when I sip a St. Charles Punch, I think about more than just how great a drink it is; I think about how great our city was, too.

Sours

UNION JACK ROSE

KIRK ESTOPINAL

The Union Jack Rose was our first runaway hit in the early days at Cure. Kirk's starting point for the drink was the classic apple brandy and grenadine sour the Jack Rose, which has a bit of a reputation as being froufrou (blame the pink color and the fact that nobody really gets apple brandy).

To bring the drink into the modern era, Kirk split the base spirit: one part Laird's apple brandy, which is an iconic American spirit and has been in production since the 1700s, and one part gin. Then he added our house-made grenadine, which is fresh and beautifully tart and completely blows the store-bought stuff out of the water. The result was an instant classic that is, in my opinion, even better than the original Jack Rose.

1 ounce (30 ml) Tanqueray gin

1 ounce (30 ml) Laird's bonded apple brandy

¾ ounce (22.5 ml) fresh lime juice

¾ ounce (22.5 ml) Grenadine (page 242)

14 drops Regans' orange bitters

3 mint leaves, including 1 for garnish

Combine all the ingredients except the garnish in a shaker filled with ice. Shake until chilled and double-strain into a coupe class. Gently slap the remaining mint leaf to release the mint oil, then place atop the drink and serve.

ST. CHARLES PUNCH

There are so many ways to make this drink, and honestly, they're all good. If you want to make a contemplative drink and really focus on the body of the brandy and port, you can build it right in the serving glass over one big ice cube. If you want something light and refreshing, shake it and pour it over crushed ice (as I suggest in the method below). Hell, it's a punch, so why not scale it up, add some dilution, and serve it party-style in a punch bowl over a giant block of ice? You'll be happy any way you do it.

1 ounce (30 ml) Infantado ruby port

1 ounce (30 ml) Pierre Ferrand 1840 cognac

¾ ounce (22.5 ml) fresh lemon juice

¾ ounce (22.5 ml) Lemon-Orange Oleo Syrup (page 243) or Cocktail & Sons Oleo Saccharum syrup

14 drops Angostura bitters

Dehydrated lemon wheel (or fresh if dried is unavailable), for garnish

Combine all the ingredients except the garnish in a shaker without ice, dry-shake, then double-strain into a double old-fashioned glass filled with crushed ice. Garnish with the lemon wheel and serve.

Sours

BRANDY CRUSTA

If I'm being honest, I'm not a huge fan of the Brandy Crusta. The juice just isn't worth the squeeze, in my opinion. But there is no denying that the Brandy Crusta is a historically relevant drink for New Orleans.

The purported inventor is Joseph Santini, who worked at the St. Louis Hotel in the 1840s. What is notable about this drink is the introduction of lemon juice—this was not common practice at the time, and it set the stage for other delicious, important drinks like the sidecar and the daisy (an inspiration for the margarita).

The Brandy Crusta was a local New Orleans drink until Jerry Thomas put it in his book. It's a cult drink now, and it was a cult drink then. I wonder if the real reason we keep talking about it is that it gives New Orleans bragging rights over the sidecar and margarita. "You know, both of those drinks can be traced back to the Brandy Crusta, and to New Orleans, the cradle of cocktail civilization. . . ." (See photos on pages 16 and 100.)

1½ ounces (45 ml) Ricou Spirits Brandy
*   Sainte Louise*

¼ ounce (7.5 ml) Cointreau

½ ounce (15 ml) Simple Syrup (page 243)

¾ ounce (22.5 ml) fresh lemon juice

1 barspoon Luxardo maraschino liqueur

7 drops Angostura bitters

Sugar, for the rim

Horse's neck lemon twist (see page 16), for
*   garnish*

Combine all the ingredients except the garnish in a shaker tin filled with ice and shake until chilled. Rim a wine glass with sugar, then pour the drink into the glass and garnish with the horse's neck lemon twist.

BASTION OF CHASTITY

TURK DIETRICH

This is arguably one of Turk's best cocktails and one that never got its due when it was on our menu. "The idea was to make a crowd-pleaser for the fall season that sneaks in some funky notes." And that's exactly what you get here. The genever, Montenegro, and Luxardo Bitter are all assertive, intense ingredients on their own. But when you combine them and add some lemon juice, you end up with a lovely, extremely pleasing autumnal sour, for those rare New Orleans days when the temperature drops below 70°F (20°C).

¾ ounce (22.5 ml) Bols genever

¾ ounce (22.5 ml) Amaro Montenegro

¾ ounce (22.5 ml) Luxardo Bitter Rosso

¾ ounce (22.5 ml) fresh lemon juice

¼ ounce (7.5 ml) Simple Syrup (page 243)

14 drops Peychaud's bitters

Freshly grated cinnamon, for garnish

Combine all the ingredients except the garnish in a shaker filled with ice. Shake until chilled and double-strain into a cocktail glass. Garnish with the cinnamon and serve.

BASTION OF CHASTITY

NEW KIND OF WATER

NEW KIND OF WATER

KIRK ESTOPINAL

"At Cure, and at most cocktail bars, you peel a million oranges but don't really have a lot of use for the juice. That was definitely a driver for me creating this drink—to use up a full ¾ ounce (22.5 ml) of juice." Readers at home may not have the same consideration (unless they have a particularly productive orange tree), but it's still a damn tasty drink and worth making. Kirk describes this as a sort of juicy Lillet Old-Fashioned. Steen's cane vinegar is a classic Louisiana ingredient (their cane syrup has been in production since 1910) that adds an acid backbone to the drink, since orange juice's acidity fluctuates so much. A sherry vinegar could work as a substitution.

Cane vinegar, for the rim

2 ounces (60 ml) Lillet Blanc

¾ ounce (22.5 ml) fresh orange juice

½ ounce (15 ml) St-Germain elderflower liqueur

7 drops Angostura bitters

Lemon peel

Rim the edge of a chilled double old-fashioned glass with vinegar then fill it with ice. Combine the Lillet, orange juice, St-Germain, and bitters in a shaker filled with ice and shake until chilled. Double-strain into the prepared cocktail glass, then express the lemon peel over the drink, discard it, and serve.

CRUTCH COCKTAIL

RICKY GOMEZ

Ricky is one of the most technically skilled bartenders I've worked with and was such an important early influence on Cure. He has since moved on to open the terrific Cuban-inspired bar Palomar in Portland, Oregon. But we still implement a lot of his best practices, especially when it comes to interacting with guests. This equal-parts cocktail is simple and elegant and close in spirit to the classic gin-Cointreau-Lillet sour, the Corpse Reviver #2, minus the anise rinse.

¾ ounce (22.5 ml) Ricou Spirits Brandy Sainte Louise

¾ ounce (22.5 ml) St-Germain elderflower liqueur

¾ ounce (22.5 ml) Dubonnet Rouge Grand Aperitif

¾ ounce (22.5 ml) fresh lemon juice

Combine all the ingredients in a cocktail shaker filled with ice and shake until chilled. Strain into a chilled cocktail glass and serve.

Sours

THE BANANA STAND

RYAN GANNON

Ryan's a great guy, but he does love to mess with people. So when he learned that one of our bartenders *hated* bananas—to the point where he was physically revolted by them—Ryan decided to put this on the menu. Since we so rarely feature vodka drinks, and since they're still so popular, Ryan knew that the Banana Stand would get ordered all the time and the poor sap would have to keep making banana syrup. Too bad for him, since this drink is delicious.

1½ ounces (45 ml) Sobieski vodka

¾ ounce (22.5 ml) Banana Syrup (recipe follows)

½ ounce (15 ml) fresh lemon juice

¼ ounce (7.5 ml) fresh lime juice

¼ ounce (7.5 ml) Giffard crème de banane liqueur

3 spritzes Angostura bitters, for garnish

Combine all the ingredients except the garnish in a shaker with 2 cubes of ice. Whip-shake, then strain into a double old-fashioned glass filled with crushed ice. Spritz the bitters from an atomizer over the drink to garnish and serve.

Banana Syrup

MAKES 2 CUPS (480 ML)

1 very ripe banana, peeled and chopped

2 cups (480 ml) Simple Syrup (page 243)

In a nonreactive container, combine the chopped banana and one-half of the peel with the simple syrup. Infuse at room temperature for 24 hours, then fine-strain into another nonreactive container. Refrigerate for up to 1 week.

NERVOUS LIGHT OF SUNDAY

MICHAEL YUSKO

According to Mike, I came in one day at the beginning of his shift and told him he had until midnight to come up with a new drink. "I'd been working there for a couple months, and although I had been bartending for fifteen years, the idea of creating a cocktail seemed as daunting as having a couple hours to whip up a COVID vaccine," he says. "So I relied on my talents at math and thievery and took the specs from one of our Cure originals, El Paraiso (page 117), and turned it around a bit. My favorite cocktail is a proper Negroni. I figured if I soured it up, subbed the Luxardo Bitter we'd been shooting after shifts for Campari, and dropped in some bitters, it couldn't turn out all that bad. At midnight, Neal rolled in with Kirk, who took one sip and said it was the most Violet Hour cocktail he'd tasted in post-Katrina New Orleans. I was immediately crowned a genius mixologist, and the rest is history."

1½ ounces (45 ml) Tanqueray gin

¾ ounce (22.5 ml) Luxardo Bitter Rosso

1 ounce (30 ml) fresh lemon juice

½ ounce (15 ml) Simple Syrup (page 243)

14 drops Bittermens hopped grapefruit
    bitters

14 drops Regans' orange bitters

Grapefruit peel, for garnish

Combine all the ingredients except the garnish in a shaker filled with ice. Shake until chilled and double-strain into a double old-fashioned glass filled with ice. Garnish with the grapefruit peel and serve.

Sours

EL PARAISO

EL PARAISO

RHIANNON ENLIL

This drink was a huge hit in the early days of Cure. Damiana is a Mexican liqueur made from a wild shrub that grows in Mexico and Central America. "It's herbal and honey-sweet, and there isn't really a substitute," Rhiannon explains. "If anything, it reminds me of yellow Chartreuse, but softer and with an interesting bitter finish." Rhiannon used the classic cocktail the Champs-Élysées as her template, subbing overproof gin for the brandy and damiana for the green Chartreuse.

1 ounce (30 ml) Hayman's Royal Dock navy-strength gin

½ ounce (15 ml) Guaycura damiana liqueur

½ ounce (15 ml) Simple Syrup (page 243)

1 ounce (30 ml) fresh lemon juice

7 drops Fee Brothers Old Fashion bitters

Orange peel, for garnish

Combine all the ingredients except the garnish in a shaker filled with ice and shake until chilled. Double-strain into a double old-fashioned glass filled with ice, garnish with the orange peel, and serve.

SUSUDARA

KIRK ESTOPINAL

Before joining the team at Cure, Kirk worked at the groundbreaking Chicago bar the Violet Hour. There, Toby Maloney created an iconic cocktail called the Poor Liza with pear eau-de-vie and green Chartreuse. It tasted uncannily like biting into a fresh pear. Kirk was interested in recreating that intense pear moment, but he wanted to get there in a different way.

1½ ounces (45 ml) Clear Creek pear eau-de-vie

¾ ounce (22.5 ml) fresh lemon juice

½ ounce (15 ml) St-Germain elderflower liqueur

½ ounce (15 ml) Simple Syrup (page 243)

21 drops Angostura bitters, plus 3 drops for garnish

Combine all the ingredients except the garnish in a shaker filled with ice. Shake until chilled, then double-strain into a chilled cocktail glass. Garnish with the 3 drops of bitters and serve.

Sours

BLACK FLAMINGO

ALEX ANDERSON

Alex used the classic tiki drink the Nui Nui as her jumping-off point but subbed Scandinavian aquavit for the rum and grapefruit for orange juice. The result is what you might call "autumn tropical," with fall flavors like honey and myrtle berry, which to me is like a juicy and fruity juniper berry with hints of rosemary and eucalyptus. "I think I originally described this cocktail as a 'refreshing drink not meant for the pool, but rather for curling up next to a fire during winter solstice and allowing the dark spirits to enter your soul.'" Mirto is a Sardinian myrtle liqueur, also featured in the Fall in Sardinia (page 148). While nothing is quite like mirto, a sloe or damson gin could work as a substitute.

1 ounce (30 ml) O.P. Anderson aquavit

¼ ounce (7.5 ml) Wild Sardinia mirto liqueur

¼ ounce (7.5 ml) Hamilton pimento dram

¼ ounce (7.5 ml) Clairin Vaval Haitian rum

½ ounce (15 ml) fresh lime juice

½ ounce (15 ml) fresh grapefruit juice

½ ounce (15 ml) Honey Syrup (page 243)

Mint sprig, for garnish

Combine all the ingredients except the garnish in a shaker tin without ice and dry-shake for 30 seconds. Double-strain into a collins glass filled with crushed ice, garnish with the mint sprig, and serve.

BEES FOR PÉLÉ

RHIANNON ENLIL

This drink is a variation on the classic daisy template. A daisy is basically booze, citrus, sweetener, and cordial. In this case, the cordial is Chartreuse, which nods to Charles Baker's 1939 Daisy de Santiago recipe. There are many layers to the name of this drink. First, there's a callback to a Bee's Knees, the classic cocktail of gin, honey, and lemon. Then there's the fact that Rhiannon uses a rhum agricole from Martinique, home to a large volcano called Mount Pelée. Last, there's a musical reference. "The guys controlled the music we played in the bar, and it was always some obscure, ambient, New York-meets-Berlin kind of energy. But I was not a cool kid in school; I spent my youth buried in Tori Amos albums. *Boys for Pele* is a Tori Amos album, so this drink was my way of sowing a little musical discord with the guys I bartended with."

1½ ounces (45 ml) La Favorite Blanc Martinique rhum

¾ ounce (22.5 ml) yellow Chartreuse

1 ounce (30 ml) fresh lemon juice

½ ounce (15 ml) Honey Syrup (page 243)

21 drops Angostura bitters, plus 5 for garnish

Combine all the ingredients except the garnish in a shaker filled with ice. Shake until chilled and double-strain into a cocktail glass. Garnish with the 5 drops of Angostura and serve.

BLACK FLAMINGO

DUNE BUGGY

COLIN BUGBEE

This drink was, in a way, a happy accident. While Colin was experimenting with the combo of funky, fruity Smith and Cross rum and the earthy French bitter aperitif Bonal, he came to a realization: "Combining Smith and Cross and Bonal pulled out these really interesting apple notes that I never really noticed before in either of them. I ran with that and tried to make an apple cider daiquiri—but without any apple ingredients. Cinnamon syrup clung to the earthiness of Bonal, and Bitter Queens' five-spice bitters brought out the allspice notes in the rum."

¾ ounce (22.5 ml) Smith and Cross traditional Jamaican rum

¾ ounce (22.5 ml) Bonal

¾ ounce (22.5 ml) fresh lime juice

¾ ounce (22.5 ml) Cinnamon Syrup (page 242)

10 drops Bitter Queens Shanghai Shirley Chinese five-spice bitters, plus 1 spritz for garnish

Combine all the ingredients except the garnish in a shaker filled with ice and shake until chilled. Double-strain into a cocktail glass, spritz the bitters from an atomizer over the top of the drink, and serve.

MAGIC TREE

RYAN GANNON

Ryan went through a bit of a "yellow phase." With this drink, the color comes from the French gentian-flavored aperitif Suze. But the key flavor here is the Homericon, which is a Greek sap liqueur that tastes like an evergreen tree smells (and also pops up in Ryan's Day Lady on page 134). If you like gin, you'll probably like Homericon; it doesn't have juniper, but it does have that brisk, green, pleasantly resiny note—without tasting like Pine-Sol.

2 slices cucumber

1½ ounces (45 ml) Stoupakis Homeric mastiha liqueur

½ ounce (15 ml) Suze d'Autrefois liqueur

½ ounce (15 ml) Hayman's Royal Dock navy-strength gin

¾ ounce (22.5 ml) fresh lime juice

¼ ounce (7.5 ml) Simple Syrup (page 243)

7 drops Bitter Truth cucumber bitters, for garnish

Muddle the cucumber in a shaker tin. Add the remaining ingredients, except the garnish, fill with ice, and shake until chilled. Double-strain into a cocktail glass, garnish with the bitters, and serve.

CURE

MAGIC TREE

ANNENE KAYE-BERRY and JEFF BERRY on New Orleans's Connection to Tropical Cocktails

Annene Kaye-Berry and Jeff Berry are the owners and operators of Latitude 29, a tropical-themed bar and restaurant located in the French Quarter's historic Bienville House Hotel. Since 2014, Annene and Jeff have served up some of the best exotic cocktails in the country: classics of the mid-century tiki canon like the Mai Tai, Zombie, and Nui Nui, as well as fantastic originals made with fresh ingredients and high-quality spirits. That said, they did make my life a living hell by naming one of their originals the "Kea Colada" after my wife, Kea, who is their lawyer. Now whenever I create a new drink I get to hear things like, "Isn't it interesting that *you* never named a cocktail after me . . ." To which I have to respond, "Well, Annene and Jeff are much nicer people than I am."

    I chatted with Annene and Jeff about New Orleans's often overlooked connection to the history of tiki, and why contemporary New Orleanians seem to be such big fans of tropical cocktails.

How did New Orleans influence tropical-drink or "tiki" culture, and vice versa?

When we talk about "tropical drinks" in the cocktail world, we're generally referring to drinks from the Caribbean, and that Holy Trinity of rum, lime, and sugar.

    New Orleans was a part of that because, as far back as the eighteenth century, New Orleans was a part of the Caribbean sphere of influence. New Orleans is commonly called "one of the northernmost cities of the Caribbean." Historically, that is correct. Many people who left Haiti during its revolution [1791–1804] moved to New Orleans because of the French colonial connection. Before that, the Spanish were a huge presence in New Orleans, which tied the city to many other Caribbean islands (most were Spanish colonies before the English, French, and Dutch moved in). If you look at the architecture, the food, the music of New Orleans—everything from voodoo to brass music—it's all connected to the African diaspora and colonial French and Spanish interests in the Caribbean.

    Rum was a product of the Caribbean. It was invented in Barbados, as far as we know, and it very quickly became a commodity in New Orleans, shortly after the city was founded in 1718. It was called *tafia*, a sort of a white moonshine made from fresh-pressed sugarcane juice that was distilled. People were drinking rum here from the very beginning.

    And of course, they were making cocktails with it—they were just calling it "punch," since the word "cocktail" didn't really exist back then. One of those proto-cocktails was what we now call the Planter's Punch (page 126), that basic Caribbean trinity of rum, lime, and sugar.

Planter's Punch is considered a building block of what we now call tropical or "tiki" drinks. How did we get from eighteenth-century Caribbean punches to the tiki craze of the mid-twentieth century?

Donn the Beachcomber [aka Donn Beach, born Ernest Raymond Gantt, who is widely considered the founding father of tiki]. Donn claimed that he was born in New Orleans, although census records show he was born in Mexia, Texas. But his parents worked in hotels in New Orleans before they moved to Texas, and his grandfather had a ranch in Mandeville [a town across Lake Pontchartrain from New Orleans]. When Donn was a teenager, he traveled the Caribbean in a yacht his grandfather owned, which is where he learned about tropical drinks and how to mix rum, lime, and sugar.

In Havana, he learned how to make a daiquiri, which was Cuban rum, lime, and sugar. In Jamaica, he learned how to make a Planter's Punch, which was Jamaican rum, lime, and sugar. In Martinique he learned how to make a ti' punch, which was Martinique rum, lime, and sugar.

When he opened up a bar after Prohibition [what is widely considered to be the first "tiki bar," Don the Beachcomber, which was in Los Angeles], he went with a Polynesian theme, because that's where the cultural zeitgeist was back in 1933. (Polynesia was considered an exotic "new" frontier; Katherine Routledge had just exposed America and Europe to the giant statues of Easter Island, and Hawaii became a tourist destination that mainland Americans could reach by steamship for the first time.) The drinks at Donn's bar, which he called "Rhum Rhapsodies," had Polynesian-themed names to go with the decor and music—but they all followed the Caribbean template of rum, lime, and sugar. Donn's great innovation?

Instead of just one citrus in a Planter's Punch, he added grapefruit and orange to the lime. He did the same thing with the sweet element: instead of just sugar, he infused sugar with cinnamon and added a little pomegranate-flavored grenadine and falernum (a complicated compound syrup of almond, ginger, lime, et al.) to that. He was basically taking every ingredient of the three-ingredient Caribbean formula and squaring or cubing it.

His true genius lies in the spirit part of the formula. He took rums of different body, character, strength, and density and mixed them together to create a base spirit that you couldn't get from any single bottle. For example, he would take a white Puerto Rican rum, which is a drier, more floral style, and mix it with a dark Jamaican rum, which is heavy and dense with a high ester content and all those impurities that make rum interesting. Then he'd take a smoky, charred wood–tasting rum from Guyana and put that on top.

This idea of taking a bunch of hyper-regional products—especially Caribbean products with French, Spanish, and English colonial ties—and combining them into a new, unique product . . . that sounds very New Orleans to me. Almost like Donn's drinks were a cocktail gumbo. This is speculation, but maybe the reason combining Puerto Rican, Jamaican, Cuban, and other Caribbean drinking traditions into one didn't seem crazy to Donn is because he spent time in New Orleans growing up.

We can only hypothesize, because there is really no record of this. But he did grow up in a place that had not totally lost touch with its cocktail culture—and had a very unique cocktail culture, at that. Maybe that influenced the imagination and scope of his work. We know New Orleans was on Donn's mind when he opened Don the Beachcomber, because he had a Sazerac on his first menu!

What about the other "founding father" of tiki, Trader Vic (aka Victor Bergeron)?

Vic also has a connection to New Orleans. When he decided to go into the tiki business himself (i.e., to rip off Don the Beachcomber), he did what Don did: He went to the Caribbean. He took the train from his home in Oakland with his wife, Esther, and their first stop was New Orleans. He learned about New Orleans drinks at the Bon Ton Café on Magazine Street, which only closed a couple of years ago. There, the head bartender, Albert Martin, taught Vic how to make rum drinks, specifically a drink called the Rum Ramsey that really left an impression. From there, Vic went on to Trinidad and Jamaica and, instead of just copying Donn's drinks (which is what most other people did), he came up with his own: the Mai Tai, Scorpion, and Fog Cutter, among many others.

How did New Orleans respond to the "tiki craze"?

By the 1950s, just about every city in the U.S. had at least one tiki place. Here in New Orleans, it was the Pontchartrain Beachcomber, an expensive white-tablecloth restaurant where people went for weddings, receptions, graduation parties—that sort of thing. Donn sued them over the name, so they changed it to the Bali Hai. In the St. Charles Hotel (see page 107), they opened up the Outrigger, another high-end place. The Fontainebleau Hotel had the Hawaiian Luau Room; there was the Hukilau in Metairie; I believe there was even a Polynesian bar in the Hotel Monteleone.

It seems like tiki really soaked into the city.

Well, it was a natural fit. In the beginning at Latitude 29, when we would go to a table, there would always be somebody in the party who'd say, "I don't really drink rum." All we'd have to do is make that old joke: "Well, you're in the northernmost city of the Caribbean, so why not give it a try?" Seventy-five percent of the time, they'd order a rum drink. It helps that one of the most famous drinks here, the Hurricane, is a rum drink. And then of course there's frozen daiquiri culture (see page 141), even if the daiquiris you get at drive-thrus are made with Everclear instead of rum.

It makes sense that people in New Orleans today are so open to the tropical drink experience. The thing about New Orleans is, we don't really let anything go: We still had collective memories from the height of the tiki craze, which were helped by our obsession with daiquiris and Hurricanes. When you guys finally opened Latitude 29, we were ready for a tropical drink renaissance!

Sours

125

PLANTER'S PUNCH

I've never been a big tiki guy. But since the two founding fathers of the tiki movement, Donn Beach and Vic Bergeron (aka Trader Vic), have such strong New Orleans connections, and since New Orleans was for centuries considered the northernmost port of the Caribbean, it seemed like a good idea to include this foundational Caribbean punch recipe. See pages 123–25 for more on the New Orleans link to tiki.

1 ounce (30 ml) Brugal Añejo rum

1 ounce (30 ml) Hamilton gold rum

1 ounce (30 ml) fresh lime juice

½ ounce (15 ml) Demerara Syrup (page 242)

21 drops Angostura bitters

Freshly grated nutmeg, for garnish

Pinch cayenne, for garnish

Dehydrated lime wheel, for garnish

Combine all the ingredients except the garnishes in a shaker filled with ice. Quick-shake, then double-strain into a footed pilsner glass filled with crushed ice. Garnish with the nutmeg, cayenne, and lime wheel and serve.

AMERICAN COUSIN

RYAN GANNON

Ryan describes this as "a mai tai but weird," following the traditional Trader Vic mai tai spec of 2 ounces (60 ml) spirit, ¾ ounce (22.5 ml) citrus juice, ½ ounce (15 ml) orange liqueur, and ¼ ounce (7.5 ml) each of orgeat and sweetener. Ryan splits the base between Scotch and almond grappa (which he knew would complement the almondy orgeat), subs orangey Gran Classico for the more traditional curaçao, then uses a bit more orgeat and grapefruit juice to sweeten it. Ryan named the drink after the movie *American Cousins*, which is about some Mafia guys who are forced to hide out in Scotland.

1 ounce (30 ml) Monkey Shoulder blended malt Scotch

1 ounce (30 ml) Nardini Mandorla

¾ ounce (22.5 ml) fresh lime juice

½ ounce (15 ml) Tempus Fugit Gran Classico bitter

½ ounce (15 ml) Orgeat (page 243)

¼ ounce (7.5 ml) fresh grapefruit juice

Mint sprig, for garnish

Combine all the ingredients except the garnish in a shaker filled with ice. Shake until chilled and double-strain into a double old-fashioned glass filled with ice. Garnish with the mint sprig and serve.

AMERICAN COUSIN

LITTLE BOOTS

LITTLE BOOTS

RYAN GANNON

Ryan describes this as a "tiki-style drink that won't knock you on your ass." I love this drink and always come back to it. By combining the tiki bitters and orgeat, Ryan creates what he calls an "à la minute Falernum." Falernum is an essential tiki ingredient but also hard to find and a pain in the ass to make, so his hack is much appreciated. The recipe calls for Diplomatico's blanco bottling, but their darker, aged reserva works great here, too.

1 ounce (30 ml) Diplomatico blanco rum

1 ounce (30 ml) Amaro Montenegro

¾ ounce (22.5 ml) fresh lemon juice

½ ounce (15 ml) Orgeat (page 243)

½ teaspoon (2.5 ml) Bittermens 'Elemakule Tiki bitters

7 drops Angostura bitters, for garnish

Lemon peel, for garnish

Combine all the ingredients except the garnishes in a shaker with 2 cubes of ice. Whip-shake, then strain into a collins glass filled with crushed ice. Garnish with the Angostura bitters and lemon peel and serve.

DEVIL'S KNEE

MORGAN SULLIVAN

"We often hear the request, 'Give me a daiquiri, but make it funky,'" Morgan explains. "Typically that translates to Jamaican rums or rhum agricoles and the musty aroma of over-ripened tropical fruit. My goal with the Devil's Knee was to deliver funk in a style that was dry, clean, and bright." So instead of looking to the Caribbean, Morgan pulled a bottle of Mexican charanda, a grassy, vegetal sugarcane-based spirit from the state of Michoacán. When paired with the Alpine amaro Braulio and a pear eau-de-vie, "the resulting flavor is green and zesty, quite savory, with notes of papaya, cooling mint, and a crisp pear finish."

1½ ounces (45 ml) Uruapan charanda blanco

½ ounce (15 ml) Clear Creek pear brandy

¾ ounce (22.5 ml) fresh lemon juice

½ ounce (15 ml) Braulio amaro

½ ounce (15 ml) Demerara Syrup (page 242)

7 drops Bitter Truth aromatic bitters

Combine all the ingredients in a shaker filled with ice and shake until chilled. Double-strain into a cocktail glass and serve.

Sours

DEFEND ARRACK

MAKSYM PAZUNIAK

Not many Americans are familiar with arrack, the base spirit in this cocktail. Like rum, arrack is distilled from sugarcane—and in the case of Batavia arrack, the bottle we use at Cure, a bit of fermented red rice. Arrack is an incredibly old spirit: It originates in South Asia and, according to historians, predates rum production in the Caribbean, making it a sort of proto-rum.

When Haus Alpenz started importing Batavia arrack to the United States, a lot of bartenders didn't know what to do with it. But Maks, who was one of our opening bartenders at Cure and now co-owns the bar Jupiter Disco in Brooklyn, is the type of guy who's always up for a challenge. He created this daiquiri variation with apricot liqueur and allspice dram and won a bunch of arrack converts in the process. For anyone who loves a daiquiri with a funky Jamaican rum like Wray & Nephew, this drink is for you.

1½ ounces (45 ml) Van Oosten Batavia arrack

¾ ounce (22.5 ml) Giffard apricot liqueur

¾ ounce (22.5 m.) fresh lime juice

½ teaspoon (2.5 ml) St. Elizabeth's allspice dram

Orange peel

Combine all the ingredients except the orange peel in a shaker filled with ice and shake until chilled. Double-strain into a cocktail glass, then express the orange peel over the drink, discard it, and serve.

CARNIVAL TIME

RHIANNON ENLIL

Rhiannon describes this as a "really delicious cachaça sour that when made right, has a sort of layered effect—golden green and then purple from the red wine on top—that matches the colors of Carnival." Layering a drink may sound complicated, but as Rhiannon points out, "gravity wants to help you, since sugary liqueurs like Chartreuse will sink to the bottom." If you want to play it extra safe, you can hold a spoon upside down over the surface of the drink and slowly pour the red wine over the back of the spoon. This will help the wine disperse evenly over the surface of the drink.

1½ ounces (45 ml) Avuá Prata cachaça

1 ounce (30 ml) fresh lime juice

½ ounce (15 ml) Ginger Syrup (page 242)

½ ounce (15 ml) green Chartreuse

¼ ounce (7.5 ml) Simple Syrup (page 243)

½ ounce (15 ml) Tempranillo, or another medium-to-full-bodied red wine, to top

Lime peel, for garnish

Combine all the ingredients except the Tempranillo and garnish in a shaker filled with ice and shake until chilled. Double-strain into a double old-fashioned glass filled with crushed ice, then slowly float the Tempranillo on top of the drink. Garnish with the lime peel and serve.

SHAKEDOWN STREET

SHAKEDOWN STREET

RHIANNON ENLIL

As so often happens, this was one of those moments where Cure bartenders decided to riff on each other's drinks. Maks had created something called the Deadhead, so-named because Kirk told him the herbaceous drink "tasted like some hippie shit." Rhiannon remembers being "tickled by the descending order of the spec—2 ounces (60 ml), ¾ ounce (22.5 ml), ½ ounce (15 ml), ¼ ounce (7.5 ml). Now I see it as just any easy formula to memorize, but at the time it struck me as a sort of decrescendo." So Rhiannon did some plug-and-play, swapping out ingredients until she found a combo that worked. "Cucumber and Aperol want to be together; cucumber and tequila want to go together . . . it came together naturally."

2 cucumber wheels, including 1 for garnish

2 ounces (60 ml) El Jimador blanco tequila

¾ ounce (22.5 ml) fresh lemon juice

½ ounce (15 ml) Aperol

¼ ounce (7.5 ml) Agave Syrup (page 242)

Muddle 1 cucumber wheel in a shaker tin. Add the remaining ingredients except the garnish, fill with ice, and shake until chilled. Double-strain into a cocktail glass, garnish with the cucumber wheel, and serve.

SUMMER IN ST. TROPEZ

TURK DIETRICH

This is Turk's most popular drink, and one that we've featured at both Cure and Vals. "My goal going in was to create a bold, herbal tequila sour. And honestly, I think this might be the best one in the world." Fighting words, but I can't say I disagree. This is a great drink. If you can't find the El Tesoro, most quality blanco tequilas will work here. The one thing you can't skip is the Old Fashion bitters. "Without those, this drink is a five out of ten, almost a disaster. With them it's a ten. Those seven drops change everything: They bridge the bitter and herbal elements and round everything out."

1 ounce (30 ml) El Tesoro platinum tequila

1 ounce (30 ml) Cynar

¾ ounce (22.5 ml) fresh lime juice

½ ounce (15 ml) yellow Chartreuse

¼ ounce (7.5 ml) Demerara Syrup (page 242)

7 drops Fee Brothers Old Fashion bitters

Grapefruit peel, for garnish

Combine all the ingredients except the garnish in a shaker filled with ice and shake until chilled. Double-strain into a double old-fashioned glass filled with ice, garnish with the grapefruit peel, and serve.

Sours

BERLIN IN THE '70s

BILLY DOLLARD

When asked about the name, Billy tells me that Maks, who was about to leave Cure to open his own bar in New York, was "excited to name his next drink New York in the '70s. I decided to steal his good idea on his way out. I chose Berlin over New York because a few weeks prior, a rowdy bunch of Germans came into Cure and ordered shots of tequila and mezcal with cinnamon-dusted orange wedges instead of salt and lime." This is also a great drink to make after a recipe that calls for an orange peel (e.g., a Manhattan) when you have some peeled oranges lying around, ready to juice.

1 ounce (30 ml) Sombra mezcal

1 ounce (30 ml) El Jimador blanco tequila

1 ounce (30 ml) fresh orange juice

½ ounce (15 ml) fresh lemon juice

½ ounce (15 ml) Cinnamon Syrup (page 242)

Orange slice, for garnish

7 drops Fee Brothers Old Fashion bitters, for garnish

Combine all the ingredients except the garnishes in a shaker filled with ice. Shake until chilled and double-strain into a double old-fashioned glass filled with ice. Garnish with the orange slice and bitters and serve.

DAY LADY

RYAN GANNON

Here's another from Ryan's "yellow phase," when he went through a bit of an obsession with yellow liqueurs, including Strega. The saffron-hued Italian liqueur showed up in a lot of his drinks. The Day Lady is a really interesting sour that looks striking in the glass. Homericon is a piney liqueur that also makes an appearance in Ryan's Magic Tree (page 120).

2 spritzes Herbsaint

1½ ounces (45 ml) Cabeza blanco tequila

¾ ounce (22.5 ml) Strega

¾ ounce (22.5 ml) fresh lemon juice

¼ ounce (7.5 ml) Agave Syrup (page 242)

1 barspoon Stoupakis Homeric mastiha liqueur

Lemon peel

Spritz a chilled cocktail glass with 2 spritzes of Herbsaint from an atomizer. Combine the remaining ingredients except the lemon peel in a shaker filled with ice and shake until chilled. Double-strain into the prepared glass, then express the lemon peel over the drink, discard it, and serve.

BERLIN IN THE '70S

CULTURE VULTURE

NEAL BODENHEIMER

The idea here was to make an agave mai tai with mezcal and tequila. Orgeat is traditionally made with almonds, but here we made a custom version with pepitas (pumpkin seeds), an ingredient used in many regional Mexican cuisines.

1½ ounces (45 ml) El Buho mezcal

½ ounce (15 ml) Siembra Azul añejo tequila

¾ ounce (22.5 ml) Pepita Orgeat (recipe follows)

¾ ounce (22.5 ml) fresh lime juice

3 drops orange flower water

1 spritz Angostura bitters, for garnish

Mint sprig, for garnish

Combine all the ingredients except the garnishes in a shaker with 2 cubes of ice. Whip-shake, then strain into a double old-fashioned glass filled with crushed ice. Spritz the bitters from an atomizer over the drink, garnish with the mint sprig, and serve.

Pepita Orgeat

MAKES ABOUT 1½ CUPS (360 ML)

4 ounces (115 g) hulled pumpkin seeds

1½ cups (360 ml) water

1½ cups (360 ml) white sugar, or as needed

Preheat the oven to 350°F (175°C) and line a baking sheet with parchment paper. Spread the pumpkin seeds on the parchment paper and roast until very lightly toasted, 5 to 7 minutes.

Soak the toasted pumpkin seeds in the water for at least 3 hours or up to 24 hours. Transfer the seeds and water to a blender and blend until pureed. Strain through a fine-mesh sieve into a nonreactive container (discard the solids), then add an equal measure by volume of sugar and stir until dissolved. Store airtight in the refrigerator for up to 1 week.

Sours

CHAMOMILE KILT

DANNY VALDÉZ

Danny was such an important member of our early team at Cure, and he always makes delicious drinks. His starting point here was a style of cocktail called the smash, which is a whiskey sour with muddled lemon and mint. This is essentially a Scotch smash with chamomile. Danny calls for Speyside single malt here, but any pure-malt blended Scotch will work.

½ lemon

2 ounces (60 ml) Speyside single malt Scotch

¾ ounce (22.5 ml) Chamomile Simple Syrup (recipe follows)

3 or 4 mint leaves

Mint sprig, for garnish

Muddle the lemon in a shaker tin. Add the Scotch, chamomile syrup, and mint leaves, fill with ice, and shake until chilled. Double-strain into a double old-fashioned glass filled with ice, garnish with the mint sprig, and serve.

Chamomile Simple Syrup

1 part white sugar

1 part freshly brewed chamomile tea

Combine the sugar and tea in a saucepan and bring to a simmer over medium-high heat. As soon as the sugar is dissolved, remove from the heat and allow to cool. Transfer to a nonreactive container and store airtight in the fridge for up to 2 weeks.

GOOD COCKTAIL

TURK DIETRICH

"At this point, I was so sick of naming cocktails," Turk tells me. I also suspect he was sick of guests sliding up to the bar and asking for a "good cocktail," as if we were in the habit of serving bad ones! So now when anyone asks for a "good cocktail," this is what they get. Lucky for them, it's a really tasty drink, especially if you're a fan of mai tais and the combination of rum and orgeat. Nowadays, lots of people are doing updated or modernized tropical cocktails, but I like to think that this kind of presaged the "bitter tiki" trend.

1½ ounces (45 ml) Banks 7-Island golden rum

½ ounce (15 ml) Tempus Fugit Gran Classico bitter

¾ ounce (22.5 ml) fresh lemon juice

½ ounce (15 ml) Orgeat (page 243)

Combine all the ingredients in a shaker filled with ice. Shake until chilled, double-strain into a cocktail glass, and serve.

Sours

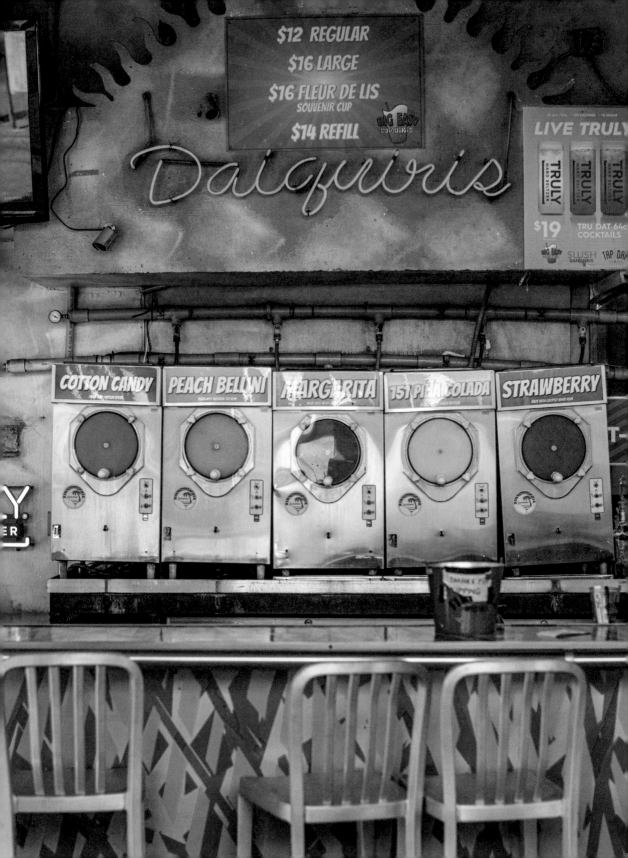

DRIVE-THRU DAIQUIRIS

Although they aren't really a big part of my life personally, I knew I couldn't write a New Orleans cocktail book without discussing frozen daiquiris. After all, they are one of the first drinks you will encounter when you set foot in the French Quarter. On Bourbon Street and surrounding it, you'll find rows of businesses with names like Big Easy Daiquiris, Daiquiri Delight, and New Orleans Original Frozen Daiquiris advertising their wares on placards and sandwich boards.

If you're a craft cocktail person, don't be fooled into thinking these have anything to do with the classic cocktail of rum, lime, and sugar. These are alcoholic Slurpees, made with grain alcohol and synthetic flavorings, with names like Banana Split and Jungle Sex.

Don't get me wrong; a Slurpee is delicious on a hot day, and an alcoholic Slurpee sounds pretty fun. When I was a rambunctious youth, I may have consumed one or two. There's something in the air in Louisiana—humidity, lax liquor laws—that makes it enticing to stroll around with a sweet, frozen libation in a giant Styrofoam cup.

Beyond Bourbon Street, once you get outside of Orleans Parish you'll find the uniquely Louisianan institution of the drive-thru daiquiri stand. This is exactly what it sounds like. It's a little stand with a window where you drive up, order an alcoholic beverage that comes in a lidded cup with a straw (I'm sure it's a total coincidence that this makes it look like a fountain soda), and drive away with it. "This can't be legal," out-of-towners always say. "Well, they put a piece of tape over the lid to close up the straw hole, so technically it's not an open container," Louisianans reply with a smile.

I actually got to meet the man credited with popularizing the drive-thru daiquiri stand, David Ervin, at a red beans and rice party at my friend Pableaux's house (see page 211). Ervin didn't invent the Louisiana-style frozen daiquiri—credit for that goes to Red and Hazel Williams, who ran a small mom-and-pop liquor store called Wilmart outside of Ruston. But Ervin was the one who decided to call the drinks "daiquiris," and he *did* come up with the brilliant idea of selling them to motorists.

As the story goes, one day in 1979, Red and Hazel Williams decided the best way to get rid of their overstock of canned Tequila Sunrise cocktails was to blend them up over ice and sell them as an impulse purchase at the counter. David Ervin was a student at Louisiana Tech in nearby Ruston at the time, and when he tasted the Williamses' cocktail, he knew it had the potential to be *big*. He secured a small business loan, and despite the skepticism of those around him, Ervin opened his drive-thru daiquiri stand in Lafayette in 1982. "Everybody told me I was an idiot," Ervin told the *Times-Picayune* in 2016. Although he had done months of independent research and concluded that there was no law explicitly prohibiting what he was about to do, Ervin feared the cops could shut him down at any time. His loan officer, convinced the business was doomed to fail, pityingly offered Ervin an extension on his first loan payment.

But customers didn't care about the legality (or not) of the operation. They didn't even care that the neon sign in front of the stand read "Drive-Thur," not "Drive-Thru." David's business was an immediate success. "It got to a point where I would drive to the store at seven o'clock in the morning, any day of the week, and there would be a line of cars at my daiquiri shop. There would be a constant line from morning until I went to sleep the following night. Most of the time I ended up just sleeping in the building," he told the *Picayune*. Three weeks after opening, Ervin walked into his bank with a brown paper bag full of cash and paid off his entire loan. A judge even ruled that the piece of Scotch tape that he used to secure the lids of his drinks was a valid solution to open-container regulations.

I have to tip my hat to David Ervin, because his business set a legal precedent that helped save my bars and restaurants during the pandemic. When we were forced to close all on-site dining and drinking in the early months of 2020, the first question I (and every bar operator) had was *Can we sell cocktails to go?* You might think that because it's New Orleans, the answer is yes. But it's actually more complicated than that. The way our liquor license works, you can walk into one of our bars, order a drink, and then decide to take the rest of that drink to go. But you have to actually order the drink on-premise. So, we asked ourselves, how are you supposed to do that if nobody's allowed in your building?

We looked around us at all the daiquiri shops that were *clearly* bars and decided our best bet was just to become a daiquiri shop. We loaded our frozen machines with Watermelon Margaritas, Frozen Coquitos, and plenty of other slushy drinks. We posted on social media that we were open for takeout and, like David Ervin before us, we waited to see if anyone would tell us that what we were doing was illegal. Nobody did, and we thanked the stars above for the frozen daiquiri loophole that allowed us to stay in business.

FROZEN DAIQUIRI

NEAL BODENHEIMER

No, I'm not giving you a recipe for a Sex on the Beach—or Jungle Juice—flavored daiquiri. Sorry, I just couldn't do it. This is inspired instead by the original frozen daiquiri, which was created in Cuba in the 1930s at the legendary bar and restaurant El Floridita. My recipe hews pretty close to the original—granulated sugar is key—but I add a dash of orange bitters. Pretty much every drink is better with bitters.

2 ounces (60 ml) Banks 5-Island rum

1 ounce (30 ml) fresh lime juice

1½ tablespoons (20 g) white sugar

7 drops Regans' orange bitters

1½ cups (360 ml) ice

Lime wheel, for garnish

Combine all the ingredients except the garnish in a blender and blend on high speed for 20 to 30 seconds. Pour into a chilled cocktail glass, garnish with the lime wheel, and serve.

CARDINALE
(PAGE 152)

CH. *5*

NEGRONIS

*Drinks with Amari and Other
Bittersweet Liqueurs*

Even though this is the shortest chapter in the book, I couldn't resist devoting some pages to the Negroni, one of my desert-island cocktails and a classic I never get tired of. I'm picky about my Negronis, though. I like them in the traditional 1-1-1 spec and get miffed when people try to sell me a 1½-¾-¾ version. My problem with those boozier Negronis is that they lose what's special about the drink. The Negroni is great because it's a hedge, in the best possible way. It's light, but also not; it's sweet, but also bitter; it's perfect for aperitivo hour, but also last call.

The Negroni doesn't necessarily have a New Orleans or even a Louisiana connection—it is Italian in origin, gained popularity among the bon vivants of Paris in the 1920s and early '30s, and found a small audience among chic American travelers to Europe after World War II. Funnily enough, the only early reference I could find to the Negroni in Louisiana newspapers was in a gossip column from the late 1950s and early 1960s in the *Shreveport Times* called "Around our Town." The writer, Viva Begbie, seems to have been a Negroni fan, because references to "the favorite drink of continental quaffers" keep popping up in her column.

Nevertheless, I knew I had to include a Negroni chapter because the drink was the launchpad for so much innovation within the contemporary craft cocktail movement. The Negroni pretty much single-handedly taught people to embrace bitterness in their drinks. These days, we take bitter flavors for granted. Nobody bats an eye when they're presented with a kale salad or third-wave drip coffee or 80 percent dark chocolate. But this was not the case fifteen years ago, and I think the Negroni deserves a lot of credit for expanding people's palates. Before the rise of the Negroni, bartenders were stuck working with strong, sweet, and sour flavors. Adding bitter to the mix was like adding a whole new color to a painter's palette.

There are only a handful of cocktails in this chapter, but I would argue that many of the most successful drinks in *other* chapters owe a debt to the Negroni. For example, in Chapter 4, Bastion of Chastity (page 110), Nervous Light of Sunday (page 115), and American Cousin (page 126) are sours by definition but lean heavily on their bitter aspects. Then there are the Manhattan variations like the Cease and Desist (page 64) and the Hardest Walk (page 69) that rely on amari (Italian bitter liqueurs) for their depth and complexity and probably wouldn't exist if bartenders in the 2000s and 2010s weren't pounding Negronis at the end of their shifts.

Once people developed a taste for bitter in their drinks, there was no turning back. And so I have to salute the Negroni—a cocktail that looks simple on paper but without which many of our Cure originals would not exist.

NEGRONI

You know what they say: If it ain't broke, don't fix it. The 1-1-1 ratio works perfectly for a Negroni, so that's the spec we use in-house. Don't mess with success!

1 ounce (30 ml) Bombay dry gin

1 ounce (30 ml) Cinzano Rosso vermouth

1 ounce (30 ml) Campari

Orange peel, for garnish

Combine all the ingredients except the garnish in a mixing glass filled with ice. Stir until chilled, then strain into a double old-fashioned glass filled with ice. Express the orange peel over the drink, place it in the glass, and serve.

4905

RYAN GANNON

Ryan calls this his "Negroni ode to Cure" (Cure's address is 4905 Freret Street). It's really a cross between a Negroni and a Manhattan, or an inverted Boulevardier with red vermouth taking the lead and cognac playing backup.

1 ounce (30 ml) Berto rosso vermouth

1 ounce (30 ml) Tempus Fugit Kina l'Aéro d'Or apéritif

½ ounce (15 ml) Tempus Fugit Gran Classico bitter

½ ounce (15 ml) Park VSOP cognac

Lemon peel, for garnish

Combine all the ingredients except the garnish in a mixing glass filled with ice and stir until chilled. Strain into a double old-fashioned glass filled with ice, garnish with the lemon peel, and serve.

Negronis

FALL IN SARDINIA

NEAL BODENHEIMER

This drink was inspired by a drink I had from my friend Chris McMillian at Revel, a variation on the "Sloe Groni"—i.e., a Negroni with rich and sweet sloe gin. When the Sardinian liqueur mirto (which also pops up in the Black Flamingo, page 118) hit the market here, I realized it would be perfect in a four-part Sloe Groni format.

¾ ounce (22.5 ml) Wild Sardinia mirto liqueur

¾ ounce (22.5 ml) Botanica barrel-finished gin

½ ounce (15 ml) Alessio Chinato vermouth

½ ounce (15 ml) Campari

Lemon peel

Combine all the ingredients except the lemon peel in a mixing glass filled with ice and stir until chilled. Strain into a double old-fashioned glass over 1 large ice cube, then express the lemon peel over the drink and discard it. Serve.

MADAME DEVALIER

GENEVIEVE MASHBURN

This bright and delicate Negroni variation could come from only one person: Genevieve, who has an incredible palate and is therefore able to pull off really nuanced, polished drinks like this. The Madame Devalier is a balancing act: It involves two different forms of the bitter herb gentian (Cocchi Americano, which is a vermouth that uses gentian as a bittering agent, and Salers, which is a gentian liqueur). To account for all that bitterness, she uses Ransom Old Tom gin, which is sweeter than standard gin and brings the whole drink together.

1½ ounces (45 ml) Cocchi Americano Rosa Aperitivo vermouth

1 ounce (30 ml) Ransom Old Tom gin

½ ounce (15 ml) Salers Gentiane Apéritif

14 drops Regans' orange bitters

7 drops Bitter Truth aromatic bitters

Lemon peel, for garnish

Combine all the ingredients except the garnish in a mixing glass filled with ice. Stir until chilled, then strain into a double old-fashioned glass filled with ice. Express the lemon peel over the drink, place it in the glass, and serve.

CURE

MADAME DEVALIER

GHOSTS OF MY LIFE

GHOSTS OF MY LIFE

TURK DIETRICH

This cocktail is really a tribute to a single ingredient: Zucca, a rhubarb-tinged amaro that is smoky, a little fruity, and bitter. It's a natural fit for the Negroni build. This cocktail became a Cure classic, so much so that it inspired riffs of its own, mostly notably Ghosts of My Life #2 (at right).

1½ ounces (45 ml) Zucca Rabarbaro amaro

1 ounce (30 ml) Plymouth gin

½ ounce (15 ml) Campari

14 drops Regans' orange bitters

Lemon peel, for garnish

Combine all the ingredients except the garnish in a mixing glass filled with ice and stir until chilled. Strain into a double old-fashioned glass filled with ice, garnish with the lemon peel, and serve.

GHOSTS OF MY LIFE #2

BRADEN LAGRONE

This drink is Braden's reaction to a cocktail Turk had created years before, Ghosts of My Life (at left). I love that Turk's cocktail not only stood the test of time but also inspired imitation. The only change is that Braden subs bacanora, an agave spirit from the Mexican state of Sonora, for the gin.

1½ ounces (45 ml) Zucca Rabarbaro amaro

1 ounce (30 ml) Cielo Rojo bacanora

½ ounce (15 ml) Campari

14 drops Regans' orange bitters

Lemon peel, for garnish

Combine all the ingredients except the garnish in a mixing glass filled with ice and stir until chilled. Strain into a double old-fashioned glass filled with ice, garnish with the lemon peel, and serve.

Negronis

CARDINALE

RYAN GANNON

At the bar, we actually batch this drink without adding any dilution, bottle it, chill it, and serve it in three-ounce (90 ml) pours. So this is a great one to serve at parties, since you can just pour straight from the bottle instead of making drinks to order all night. (See photo on page 144.)

¾ ounce (22.5 ml) Falcon Spirits Amaro Aplomado

¾ ounce (22.5 ml) Mattei Cap Corse Blanc quinquina

¾ ounce (22.5 ml) Valdespino Amontillado sherry

½ ounce (15 ml) Cappelletti aperitivo

¼ ounce (7.5 ml) Zucca Rabarbaro amaro

7 drops citric acid

Orange peel

Combine all the ingredients except the orange peel in a mixing glass filled with ice and stir until chilled. Strain into a sherry copita or cordial glass, express and discard the orange peel, and serve.

To make a large batch, as we do at the bar, in a 750-ml bottle, mix 6 ounces (180 ml) Amaro Aplomado, 6 ounces (180 ml) quinquina, 6 ounces (180 ml) sherry, 4 ounces (120 ml) Cappelletti aperitivo, and 2 ounces (60 ml) Zucca Rabarbaro amaro and chill in the fridge for up to 3 months. To serve, pour 3 ounces (90 ml) into a sherry copita or cordial glass and express and discard an orange peel.

PALE FIRE

MORGAN SULLIVAN

"I wanted to create something bold and almost dessert-like, but also herbal, slightly bitter, and pleasing to a Negroni drinker," Morgan says of the Pale Fire. "Valdespino moscatel is probably one of my favorite products ever. It's rich, floral, chocolaty, and herbaceous. It's truly what makes this Negroni sing. I want this cocktail in the fall, after dinner, on a nighttime walk. The malt, moscatel, and soft bitter remind me: No, there is nothing wrong with yet another Negroni variation."

1 ounce (30 ml) Bols genever

¾ ounce (22.5 ml) Valdespino moscatel sherry

½ ounce (15 ml) Pierre Ferrand curaçao

¼ ounce (7.5 ml) Amaro Montenegro

14 drops Bittermens Krupnik herbal honey bitters

Lemon peel, for garnish

Combine all the ingredients except the garnish in a mixing glass filled with ice. Stir until chilled, then strain into a double old-fashioned glass filled with ice. Garnish with the lemon peel and serve.

PALE FIRE

MY MARDI GRAS DIARY

In case you were wondering, we really do take Mardi Gras seriously here. It isn't just a show we put on for tourists; it's a municipal holiday, with schools closing Friday through Wednesday of Mardi Gras week.

Technically, Mardi Gras (French for "Fat Tuesday" . . . but nobody calls it that) refers to a specific day—the Tuesday in February or March that precedes Ash Wednesday and Lent in the Christian calendar (aka Shrove Tuesday). But in Louisiana, "Mardi Gras" refers to the whole Carnival season, which, depending on who you ask, could start the Friday beforehand or as early as Twelfth Night/the Feast of the Epiphany on January 6. (Personally, I just can't get into the Carnival spirit that early in the year. Here I am, trying to set New Year's resolutions and walk the straight and narrow after a holiday season full of rich food and drink. Then along comes Twelfth Night and king cake and more cocktails. Just give me a couple of weeks to get my life back on the rails, please!)

As a native of New Orleans, I have mixed feelings about Mardi Gras. On the one hand, it's a time of joy and revelry, when we come together as a city to celebrate our collective rituals and traditions. It's a holiday that is uniquely ours and isn't celebrated this way anywhere else in the world. On the other hand, a lot of the Mardi Gras traditions have come under well-deserved scrutiny in recent years, as we try to root out the problematic and exclusionary vestiges of our past. It is not lost on me that as a Jewish man, I would have been barred from joining most Mardi Gras krewes until just a few decades ago—as were African Americans, women, and many other marginalized groups. Then there's the environmental impact of Mardi Gras, especially plastic waste from beads and litter, which wreaks havoc on the region's already struggling ecosystem. New Orleans's history is a big part of what makes the city great, but we cannot shy away from, and must work to correct, the ugly parts.

When people ask me if they should come down for Mardi Gras, my answer is always, *Yes, do it*. Everyone should get to experience it at least once. But I do think there is a right way to do Mardi Gras and a wrong way. The right way involves a bit of planning, plenty of food, lots of water, and just being a kind and respectful citizen. The wrong way involves dehydration and probably a bit of regret. Here's how I like to do it.

FRIDAY. The marquee events of Mardi Gras are the parades that take place in the days leading up to (and on) Tuesday. Social clubs called krewes host the parades: Members build (or pay people to build) elaborate floats, dress up in costume, and hand out or toss signature "throws," which people collect and obsess over to varying degrees. (For example, parade-goers will climb on top of each other to snag one of Muses' glittered stilettos or a hand-painted coconut from the krewe of Zulu.) I'm part of a krewe that rides on Friday evening. For me, it's mostly an excuse to hang out with my friends. Our tradition is to hit up Arnaud's and drink Ojen Cocktails (page 51) before we ride. This is definitely one of my favorite parts of Mardi Gras. Ojen might not be an everyday thing, but it sure as hell puts you in the mood to get in costume and strap yourself into a parade float. (Yes, we do actually strap in with safety belts, as mandated by the city of New Orleans. As someone who has needed the belt in the past, I am a big proponent of this safety measure.)

When I can get my act together, I like to make a big batch of punch, bottle it, and throw it in the ice chest that sits on the parade float. There's a very well-known New Orleans chef who rides next to me (I'd say who, but technically we're supposed to keep krewe membership confidential) and always brings bags of cheeseburgers to share, too. I love this potluck, BYO element of the ride.

We always have grand plans for dinner afterward, but if I'm being honest, I usually end up in the den of whatever hotel the krewe has rented for the evening, slamming cold roast beef sandwiches before I go home to bed. Like Icarus, I've flown too close to the sun too many times. So these days, I try to behave myself this early in the proceedings.

MARDI GRAS PUNCH

This punch is a lot like Taaka (a local vodka . . . if you know, you know): It mixes easy; just add people.

MAKES ABOUT 3 QUARTS (2.8 LITERS); SERVES 24

....

1 (750-ml) bottle Marsh House rum

1 (750-ml) bottle medium-bodied red wine

2 ounces (60 ml) Wray & Nephew white overproof rum

1 cup (240 ml) fresh lemon juice

1 cup (240 ml) Lemon-Orange Oleo Syrup (page 243)

7 dashes Angostura bitters

32 ounces (1 quart, or 960 ml) filtered water, sparkling water, or sparkling wine

Fresh or dehydrated lemon wheels, each with a few drops of Angostura bitters on top, for garnish

Combine all the ingredients except the garnish in a large punch bowl. Add a large block of ice and stir until chilled. Add additional bitters to taste if needed, garnish with the lemon wheels, and serve with a ladle in individual glasses.

SATURDAY. Saturday is my wife Kea's day to ride. Her krewe is notable because it was the first all-female krewe, founded in the early 1900s (although they didn't start parading until 1959). My daughter, Hayden, loves to watch her mom ride, so I try to pop out a bit early to set up her parade ladder so she'll get a good view.

If you're doing Mardi Gras with a kid, I highly recommend snagging a parade ladder. You can buy them online on sites like Etsy or from local hardware stores. It's basically a ladder with a little booster seat and safety rail attached on top, painted in bright colors and then tricked out with streamers, pom-poms, beads, or whatever else your heart desires. If you lived in New Orleans as a kid, memories of your Mardi Gras parade ladder probably live alongside those of your favorite Halloween costume or a beloved childhood pet. It's just something that is part of growing up here.

SUNDAY. If I'm being totally honest, by this time both Kea and I are worn out and ready for a couple of days of rest. That said, Sunday really is peak Mardi Gras bacchanalia and an all-star parade day, with the krewe of Thoth riding in the morning and Bacchus—one of the biggest and most elaborate parades of the season—later that evening. Thoth is a fun one to catch as it cuts deeper into the residential areas of Uptown than any other parade. My biggest piece of advice is to prepare to walk a lot if you plan to catch both parades. Pretty much the only way to navigate the parade lines is on foot.

You'll notice that Sunday is a big day of house parties, so see if you can find a nice local to invite you to their festivities!

MONDAY. Thank God everyone tends to agree that Lundi Gras is a more chill day—a time to recover. Lunch spots tend to be slammed as everyone scrambles to put their feet up and gather their wits, so make a reservation well in advance. The krewes of Proteus and Orpheus both ride that night, and we often make the effort to see Proteus because it's beautiful, close to our house, and super old-school. Often, we'll grab a bite at Pascale's Manale, a traditional spot that leans Italian and has been open since 1913, and get ready for the next morning (which starts early if you plan to catch Zulu, Rex, or St. Anne downtown).

Some people party straight through Lundi Gras night and make it a quick Mardi Gras day, but I'm too old for that now. (My M.G. day is quick, but not particularly debaucherous.)

TUESDAY. The oldest Mardi Gras krewe is Rex, which first paraded in 1872. Because of this history, the Rex parade is considered one of the marquee events of Mardi Gras season. My favorite thing to do is to get a pot of something going—gumbo or red beans are the obvious moves here—in the morning, so it's ready when you come back from the parade. This is the only time I am happy to live so close to a parade route, since the whole family really can just pop out, then come home in time for a big lunch.

PARADE SURVIVAL KIT

- Go-cups and a thermos full of Mardi Gras Punch (page 155).

- An ice chest of basic domestic beer and beer koozies.

- A box of Popeye's fried chicken: Don't over-think this. Popeye's may be a chain, but it's still damn delicious. Buy it the day before and refrigerate it—I swear this stuff tastes as good (if not better) cold.

- WATER. More than you think you'll need. Trust me on this one.

- Sunscreen. Duh.

- Parade ladder for any young kids.

- A home base to use the facilities when needed.

FLIPS AND FIZZES

Rich Drinks with Eggs and Dairy

People have been putting eggs and spirits together for centuries. The earliest of these concoctions were called *nogs* (as in eggnog) or *flips*, and most contained a whole egg. If that combination seems odd to you, keep in mind that back in those days, alcohol was (at least in certain contexts) considered medicinal. So why not fortify your prescription with a nutrient-rich egg, which has the added benefit of making the "medicine" go down easy?

At some point, folks decided to leave out the egg yolk and to instead froth up their cocktails with just the whites. These egg-white cocktails were descended from a popular sour category called *fizzes* (essentially a sour with seltzer), the most famous of which was the gin fizz—gin, sugar, lemon, and seltzer. In 1882, Harry Johnson published recipes for the Silver Fizz (Old Tom gin, sugar, lemon, egg white) and the Morning Glory Fizz (Scotch, sugar, lemon, lime, absinthe, egg white) in his *New and Improved Bartender's Manual.* Once egg whites entered the equation, it's easy to understand why they stuck around: They are amazing in cocktails. Egg whites contribute this perfect bit of texture but also dry a drink out. That's a balance that is hard to replicate with any other ingredient; most things that add body to a drink also add either proof or sweetness. Not so with egg whites. Egg whites have a unique molecular structure that causes them to strip things out of a liquid. If you've ever heard of an "egg-white raft" (a culinary technique where egg whites are used to clarify cloudy stock) or "fining" wine with egg whites (to remove unwanted compounds), then you understand the magic of egg whites.

The most important egg drink in the New Orleans canon is of course the Ramos Gin Fizz (page 160), which inspired many imitators in its time and inspires modern New Orleans bartenders to this day. The key to success with this and most other dairy drinks is a technique called the dry shake, where you shake certain ingredients *without* ice before adding the remaining ingredients and ice. For a more in-depth explanation of dry shaking, turn to page 14.

RAMOS GIN FIZZ

If we're going to rank New Orleans cocktails in terms of cult following, I'd stick the Ramos Gin Fizz at the top of the list. And honestly, I think it deserves all the adoration. As somebody who creates cocktails for a living, I just have to bow down to Henry Charles "Carl" Ramos (1856–1928), because his gin fizz is a mind melter. Ramos's genius is that he puts all these ingredients together that should *not* go together—egg, cream, gin, two different kinds of citrus (three if you count the orange flower water)—and somehow makes it work. Ramos was far from a one-hit wonder (I love his Pequot Fizz, page 166, for example), but even if this were the only drink he ever created, I would still consider him a legend. With his gin fizz, he caught lightning in a bottle.

Ramos's mastery extended beyond just drink creation, though. He was also a savvy businessman with excellent PR instincts and a flair for theatrics. You may have heard that the Ramos Gin Fizz takes anywhere from twelve to fifteen minutes to be shaken properly. This can be traced back to Ramos himself, who insisted on the insanely long shake. At his establishments, the Imperial Cabinet Saloon and the Stag (both in the orbit of the St. Charles Hotel, see page 107), he was said to bring in as many as thirty extra employees on busy occasions like Mardi Gras to keep up with demand (and presumably, to make sure his bartenders' arms didn't give out). I can only imagine the deafening sound of ice hitting metal as an assembly line of thirty men dutifully shook their gin fizzes. At my bar, it gets loud enough when *two* bartenders double-shake a round at the same time.

Ramos may have trained his staff to shake for a full twelve minutes, but at Cure, we've determined that two minutes and thirty seconds is totally adequate. We're able to do this thanks in part to a method called the dry shake, wherein we shake the citrus, egg white, and orange flower water without ice for thirty seconds before adding ice and the remaining ingredients. With any egg-white drink, the goal is to create a stable meringue layer that will float on top of the cocktail. Spirits, sugar, and water all impede this process, which is why when you're whipping egg whites in a stand mixer, cookbooks will tell you to wipe your bowl and beaters completely dry and add any sugar midway through the process. Citrus, by contrast, helps stabilize the egg-white foam, which is why we start with egg and citrus and add the ice, gin, simple syrup, and cream later.

I always found it odd that Ramos and his contemporaries didn't figure out the dry shake. They just combined all the ingredients in a tin over ice and went for it. But ice was not an unlimited resource in those days; it was costly and either harvested in the North and then transported by ship or train to the South or, starting in 1868, manufactured in a steam-powered mechanical ice facility on Delachaise Street. For each drink, bartenders would have had to use an ice pick to whack a hunk from the large block that sat on a tray or in an ice box behind the bar. (Or maybe they'd just rinse and reuse the same piece of ice and plop it into the next drink—I can't say I'd blame them.) So if there was a way to make the Ramos Gin Fizz faster and with less ice, a shortcut, why didn't Ramos and his staff take it? If they worked with these ingredients every day, they should have understood how to efficiently turn an egg into a meringue—it's not like this is advanced food science.

Part of me has to wonder if the decision not to stage out ingredients was a conscious choice. Maybe Ramos knew exactly what he was doing: He understood that the appeal of his drink was

the spectacle of it all and that it took a lot of time and manpower to make it right. Call it the "flair" bartending of the early 1900s.

This leads me to a maxim you may have heard about the Ramos Gin Fizz: that you should never order one if your bartender is slammed. There is some truth to that one. The main problem is that once one person orders one, all of the sudden *everyone* wants one of those tall drinks with the precariously wobbling head. At Cure, we pour our Ramoses so that a pillowy, cloud-like layer of foam teeters an inch or so above the top of the glass. It's a beautiful, delicate thing and damn hard to resist.

½ ounce (15 ml) fresh lime juice

½ ounce (15 ml) fresh lemon juice

1 medium egg white

7 drops orange flower water (see Note)

2 ounces (60 ml) London Dry gin

1 ounce (30 ml) Simple Syrup (page 243)

1½ ounces (45 ml) heavy cream

2 ounces (60 ml) soda water

Orange peel, for garnish

Combine the lime and lemon juice, egg white, and orange flower water in a shaker tin without ice and dry-shake for 30 seconds. Add the gin, simple syrup, and two 1¼-inch (3-cm) ice cubes and whip-shake for 1 minute. Add the cream and shake for 1 minute more. Bang the bottom of the tin against the countertop to settle the drink.

Add the soda water to a chilled collins glass, then slowly double-strain one-third of the contents of the tin into the glass. Bang the bottom of the tin against the countertop to settle the drink again, slowly double-strain another third of the drink into the glass, bang the tin to settle the drink once more, then slowly double-strain the remainder of the drink into the glass.

Express the orange peel on the outside of the glass and on top of the foam, then gently rest the orange peel on top of the foam (or discard it, if that's your preference) and serve with a straw.

Note: Use a medicine dropper to apply the orange flower water. If you can't find orange flower water in the baking aisle of your grocery store, look for it in Middle Eastern markets. It's one of the more ingenious aspects of Ramos's recipe and part of what separates his gin fizz from other egg-white drinks of the era. Orange flower water is a finicky ingredient that, if overused, has the potential to make cocktails cloying and perfumy. But in small doses, it adds this really enticing and unexpected floral note. If your orange flower water is really fresh and smells strong, you may wish to reduce the number of drops to three; if it's more muted, keep to seven. In the case of the Ramos Gin Fizz, it helps to tamp down the sulfurous, wet-dog smell you sometimes get from egg-white drinks. Ramos clearly understood his ingredients, which is why he was such a master bartender.

DUELING RAMOSES

Arguing about specs is a favorite hobby among modern craft cocktail bartenders, but it's hardly a new phenomenon. For proof, just turn to an article about the Ramos Gin Fizz published in the *New York Times* on July 26, 1935.

Actually, the gin fizz is more of a side player in the story. The real protagonist is Huey Long, the legendary Louisiana governor and senator whose career was cut short when he was assassinated in September 1935.

A few months before his death, Long traveled to New York to speak against FDR and his New Deal, which Long felt didn't go far enough to tax the rich and redistribute their wealth. But more interesting to the *Times* than Long's policy agenda was the "one-man circus" Long had staged in the bar of the New Yorker Hotel, "demonstrating to newspapermen, photographers, waiters, bartenders and hotel guests how to make the celebrated Ramos Gin Fizz." According to the story, "The senator did not do the mixing, but he directed the operations of Sam Guarino, head bartender of the Hotel Roosevelt at New Orleans." Guarino had "arrived from New Orleans by airplane yesterday morning in response to a hurry call from the Kingfish when the latter discovered there was no one in this city who could be trusted to mix the famous gin fizz properly."

Publicity stunt, or did Long really love the Ramos Gin Fizz so much that he needed to fly in an expert from New Orleans to fix his daily dose? Either way, the *Times* reported on the emergency bartender airlift and even printed Long's preferred recipe: "A noggin of gin, the white of an egg, two drops of orange flower water, dash of vanilla, one-half glass of milk with a little tincture of cream, pulverized sugar, a small dash of seltzer and lots of ice. Shake well for ten minutes."

Here's the part of the story I really love: Apparently, Long's antics riled up one reader so much that they decided to write a letter to the editor. But the thing that sparked W.D. Rose of Schenectady, New York, into action was *not* Long's threats of bloody revolution, nor his disparaging remarks about the president. No, it was his Ramos Gin Fizz recipe.

While the writer does not feel equal to enter into a controversy with the versatile and able Senator on any subject, much less on that of Ramos fizzes, and while not denying that the formula announced by Senator Long may be that of a perfect fizz, still the writer feels obliged to submit to the readers of the *Times* the only authentic and original formula for that famous and delectable decoction—the Ramos gin fizz:

> One tablespoon simple syrup.
> One teaspoon lemon juice.
> One jigger gin.
> Ten drops orange flower water.
> One tumbler rich milk.
> Ice well, shake one minute and strain.

W.D. Rose's recipe is notable for its lack of egg white and lime juice and for its short, one-minute shake. But for once, I'm not here to quibble about specs. What really stands out to me is that a random citizen of a midsize town in Upstate New York had such strong opinions about the Ramos Gin Fizz, they felt compelled to write in to the paper of record. To me, that says everything you need to know about the cult of the Ramos Gin Fizz and just how powerful the legacy of this drink really is.

ON HENRY RAMOS AND COCKTAILS
AS A FORCE FOR GOOD

I've always had a lot of admiration for Henry Charles Ramos, but it was only in the last few years that I started to feel a real kinship with him. In a weird way, I see some of myself in Ramos. He was the type of bar owner who wanted to be more than just a guy who sells booze. He wanted to be an investor in his community. By all accounts, he was not only a successful businessperson, but also a model citizen who was very active in his Elks Lodge and, according to one obituary, a high-ranking Freemason. Like many Masons of the era, he didn't really drink and was a teetotaler for long stretches of his life. Whereas many New Orleans bars flouted local laws that limited the sale of alcohol on Sundays, Ramos closed down for all but two hours that day. The rest of the week, the lights were off by 8 P.M. According to Elizabeth M. Williams and Chris McMillian in their book *Lift Your Spirits*, he set up a scholarship program to help young men in his neighborhood pay for school. There's an undocumented but believable story that even Carrie Nation, the Prohibition evangelist and Enemy No. 1 of bars and bartenders everywhere, was a fan of Ramos's. Allegedly she said that if every bar owner conducted themselves like Ramos, then Prohibition wouldn't have been necessary.

I can only imagine how Ramos must have felt once Prohibition was passed into law. Ramos didn't even drink; for him, cocktails and alcohol were purely business. I'm sure Ramos saw and understood the way alcohol could ravage people's lives, so he worked hard to model and encourage responsible behavior. Then, overnight, Ramos went from being a productive member of society to an outlaw. What would that have done to the psyche of a guy like him—to go from being well liked and respected to being told he was no better than a drug pusher? It doesn't surprise me that once Prohibition went into effect, Ramos never mixed another drink again.

People talk a lot about the long-term scars of Prohibition: the loss of cultural memory, the way the craft of bartending and centuries-old distilling traditions were just forgotten. But these days I can't stop thinking about the immediate loss folks like Ramos must have felt. How many Americans lost their livelihoods? How many lost their vocation, their sense of purpose? How many communities lost essential gathering spaces, those "third places" where deals are made, politics discussed, and relationships forged?

It's no coincidence that I am thinking and writing this in the midst of a pandemic that has completely decimated the American hospitality industry. When the coronavirus hit New Orleans and I was told to shut my bars down, I of course understood the health and safety reasons why I had to do so. We did not hesitate to close. But damn if I didn't feel like Ramos on the eve of Prohibition. In an instant, I had to accept that the businesses we had so lovingly and carefully built to serve our friends and neighbors were now considered a danger to those same people.

Like Henry Ramos, I've always considered bartending a business, not a lifestyle. I have a wife and kid I hurry home to each night, and even if I didn't, I don't really see myself slapping on the suspenders and porkpie hat and jetting from international cocktail convention to convention. But I care deeply about my bars. To me, they have the potential to be more than just a spot where you grab a drink; they are gathering places that are integral to the daily movements of civic life.

That's a big part of the reason why, in 2018, I agreed to become the co-chair of the Tales of the Cocktail Foundation. Tales started in 2002 as a small gathering of beverage industry people with an organized walking tour of New Orleans bars. Since then, it has blossomed into a thirty-thousand-person trade conference and festival and a rite of passage for cocktail and spirits professionals around the world. Tales breathes life into the otherwise sleepy streets of midsummer New Orleans, and as a bar owner, I know how vital it is to sustaining local bars, restaurants, and hotels (and the tens of thousands of hospitality workers they employ) during the off-season.

Today, the Tales of the Cocktail Foundation is a nonprofit that educates, advances, and supports the global hospitality industry. We're committed to tackling the tough issues facing our industry: health care and especially mental health, substance abuse, gender and racial equality, the safety of our workers and our patrons, and more.

Although it wasn't a conscious choice, you could say that my work with Tales is my way of channeling the spirit of Henry Ramos. He and I both traffic in something that is considered taboo, but we both take seriously the responsibility of selling alcohol. Our goal has always been to give back to our communities and ensure that our bars are a force for good, not ill.

When Prohibition went into effect at the stroke of midnight on January 16, 1920, Ramos put away his shakers and declared that he had mixed his last gin fizz. He retired and lived out the remaining eight years of his life quietly. The coronavirus pandemic similarly upended my businesses and my livelihood, but I have no intention of throwing in the towel just yet. Next time I see you at Cure, Vals, Cane & Table, Peychaud's, Dauphine's, or Tales of the Cocktail, I will be so happy about it. I might even shake you up a Ramos Gin Fizz to commemorate the occasion.

PEQUOT FIZZ

This one is a bit of an obscurity that Kirk uncovered and developed when he was doing research for our dearly departed cobbler bar, Bellocq. (The cobbler was one of the most popular cocktail categories of the nineteenth century, essentially a spirit or fortified wine like Madeira or sherry served over a mountain of crushed ice and garnished with fresh seasonal fruit. It's so simple, with components we take for granted now, but back in the day, it was the height of opulence. Ice! Fresh fruit! Straws! Many cobblers are naturally low-proof, which is one of the reasons we decided to dedicate an entire bar to an exploration of the category.)

It's hard to find too much about the Pequot Fizz, but it is generally attributed to Henry Ramos and first appeared in print in Geo. R. Washburne and Stanley Bronner's *Beverages de Luxe* from 1914. It's a wonderful drink, essentially a gin sour with lime instead of lemon and a bit of mint for garnish. Refreshing, drinkable—Henry Ramos has done it again.

¾ ounce (22.5 ml) fresh lime juice

1 medium egg white

1½ ounces (45 ml) London Dry gin

1 barspoon superfine sugar

Soda water, to top

Mint sprig, for garnish

Combine the lime juice and egg white in a shaker tin without ice and dry-shake for 30 seconds. Add the gin and sugar, fill the shaker with 2 large ice cubes, and shake until chilled. Double-strain into a chilled old-fashioned glass filled with ice, top with soda water, garnish with the mint sprig, and serve.

THE PERIPHERAL

TURK DIETRICH

This cocktail started as a genever Negroni, but Turk felt the ingredients weren't jibing—until he put a whole egg into it. What resulted is a really delicious, really pleasing flip, perfect for fall and winter. You might not think it at first, but egg and amaro actually go together really well.

1 medium egg

1 ounce (30 ml) Bols genever

1 ounce (30 ml) Cocchi Storico vermouth di Torino

1 ounce (30 ml) Amaro Nonino

2 spritzes Angostura bitters

Place the egg in a shaker tin without ice and dry-shake for 30 seconds. Add the genever, vermouth, and amaro to the shaker, fill the shaker with ice, and shake until chilled. Strain into a chilled cocktail glass, spray the Angostura from an atomizer over the surface of the drink, and serve.

Flips and Fizzes

ST. ROSE SOUR

RYAN GANNON

I love this drink because every ingredient has its place, and many of them do double duty. For example, Ryan decided to pair pisco and sherry since they are both grape distillates. But the sherry also helps to add an acid backbone to the drink, since grapefruit (which pairs amazingly with Galliano) is a lower-acid citrus and needs some help. This is just further proof that Ryan really is a cocktail savant who knows how to put flavors together.

¾ ounce (22.5 ml) fresh grapefruit juice

1 medium egg white

¾ ounce (22.5 ml) Inocente fino sherry

¾ ounce (22.5 ml) Macchu pisco

½ ounce (15 ml) Galliano

¼ ounce (7.5 ml) Simple Syrup (page 243)

Lemon peel

Combine the grapefruit juice and egg white in a shaker tin without ice and dry-shake for 30 seconds. Add the sherry, pisco, Galliano, and simple syrup, fill the shaker with ice, then shake until chilled. Double-strain into a chilled cocktail glass, express the lemon peel over the drink and discard it, and serve.

CRUEL SUMMER

CHRISTINA RANDO

Banana and black pepper might not seem like a natural pairing, but it really works well. People ordered it and loved it, which is all we can really hope for with any drink!

¾ ounce (22.5 ml) fresh lemon juice

1 medium egg white

1 ounce (30 ml) Hayman's Old Tom gin

½ ounce (15 ml) Ford's gin

½ ounce (15 ml) Tempus Fugit crème de banane

½ ounce (15 ml) Black Pepper Syrup (page 242)

Freshly ground black pepper, for garnish

Combine the lemon juice and egg white in a shaker tin without ice and dry-shake for 30 seconds. Add the two gins, crème de banane, and black pepper syrup, fill the shaker with ice, and shake until chilled. Strain into a chilled coupe glass, garnish with a crank of fresh black pepper, and serve.

CURE

ST. ROSE SOUR

BEYOND THE INFINITE

TURK DIETRICH

If you've never tried Bonal, a bitter, spicy gentiane, this is a good place to start. The orange notes from the Cointreau pair really nicely with the earthiness of the Bonal, which on its own is quite bitter and intense. (I like to tell people that this drink is as mainstream as Bonal gets.) Beyond the Infinite drinks like an earthy, herbal whiskey sour, with plenty of fizz from the soda water to lighten and brighten it.

Combine all the ingredients except the soda water and bitters in a shaker tin filled with ice and shake until chilled. Double-strain into a Delmonico glass, top with the soda water, and spray the Angostura from an atomizer over the top of the drink. Serve.

1 ounce (30 ml) Bonal

½ ounce (15 ml) Buffalo Trace bourbon

½ ounce (15 ml) Cointreau

½ ounce (15 ml) fresh lemon juice

½ ounce (15 ml) Simple Syrup (page 243)

1 medium egg white

½ ounce (15 ml) soda water

1 spritz Angostura bitters

CURE

IRISH GOODBYE

MATT LOFINK

Matt describes this as a dry, not-too-sweet, "very crushable" whiskey sour. Fennel and peach is an unexpected but delicious flavor pairing that works amazingly well with the spice notes of the whiskey.

¾ ounce (22.5 ml) fresh lemon juice

1 medium egg white

1½ ounces (45 ml) Tullamore D.E.W. Irish whiskey

¼ ounce (7.5 ml) Giffard crème de pêche liqueur

¼ ounce (7.5 ml) Fennel Syrup (recipe follows)

4 mint leaves

10 drops Peychaud's bitters, for garnish

Mint sprig, for garnish

Combine the lemon juice and egg white in a shaker tin without ice and dry-shake for 30 seconds. Add the whiskey, pêche liqueur, fennel syrup, and mint leaves to the shaker tin, fill the shaker with ice, and shake until chilled. Double-strain into a double old-fashioned glass filled with ice. Dot the bitters on the surface of the drink, then use a toothpick or cocktail straw to swirl the bitters in an attractive pattern. Garnish with the mint sprig and serve.

Fennel Syrup

MAKES ABOUT 2 CUPS (480 ML)

2 tablespoons fennel seeds

2 cups (480 ml) hot (190 to 200°F/88 to 93°C) water

2 cups (400 g) white sugar

In a small skillet over medium heat, toast the fennel seeds until fragrant, 1 to 2 minutes. Transfer to a bowl, add the water, and infuse until the water is cool. Add the sugar, stir until dissolved, then fine-strain and store in the refrigerator for up to 4 weeks.

Flips and Fizzes

MAYBE, BABY

MATT LOFINK

Matt has a talent for taking out-of-fashion, lame cocktails and updating them for the modern palate. On one of our slower nights, a bartender challenged Matt to make "the best lemon drop ever." This is what he came up with: a flip with a whole egg and Acqua di Cedro, a delicious grappa that practically tastes like lemon curd. If you like limoncello, this drink is for you.

1 medium egg

1 ounce (30 ml) Boyd and Blair potato vodka

1 ounce (30 ml) Acqua di Cedro

½ ounce (15 ml) Simple Syrup (page 243)

3 drops Saline Solution (page 243)

Lemon peel, for garnish

Place the egg in a shaker tin without ice and dry-shake for 30 seconds. Add the vodka, Acqua di Cedro, simple syrup, and saline solution to the shaker, fill the shaker with ice, and shake until chilled. Double-strain into a Delmonico glass, garnish with the lemon peel, and serve.

JASON'S ASCENSION

TURK DIETRICH

By his own admission, Turk rarely sets out to make crowd-pleasing cocktails, at least not intentionally. Accessibility was just never a high priority. But with this drink, he wanted to challenge himself to create something that everyone would like. It worked. "I knew that the fruity notes of the pisco paired really well with the chamomile of the La Gitana manzanilla sherry. Using grenadine instead of simple syrup is an option worth considering if you're looking to add another layer of delightful fruitiness." Crude is a small-batch bitters operation based out of Raleigh, North Carolina; if you can't find it in stores, you can buy it online.

¾ ounce (22.5 ml) fresh lemon juice

1 medium egg white

1 ounce (30 ml) Macchu pisco

1 ounce (30 ml) La Gitana manzanilla sherry

½ ounce (15 ml) Grenadine (page 242)

14 drops Crude Bitterless Marriage
   hibiscus-lavender-oak bitters

3 drops Angostura bitters, for garnish

Combine the lemon juice and egg white in a shaker tin without ice and dry-shake for 30 seconds. Add the pisco, sherry, grenadine, and hibiscus-lavender-oak bitters to the shaker, fill with ice, and shake until chilled. Strain into a chilled cocktail glass and dot the Angostura over the surface of the drink. Use a toothpick or cocktail straw to connect the drops and form a swirl pattern, then serve.

Flips and Fizzes

CAFÉ ITALO

CAFÉ ITALO

KIRK ESTOPINAL

This drink is my sister Carey's favorite Cure cocktail. It hasn't been on the menu for years, but every time she visits town, which happens once or twice a year, she comes in and orders this rich, orangey flip. Cure has never served coffee, but this is kind of our nod to the flavors and experience of an after-dinner coffee. Kirk says he was inspired by the Terry's brand chocolate oranges—"you know, the kind you used to smash on the ground"—his mom used to get him as a kid. Here, shaking the drink with an orange peel in the tin contributes a juicy orange flavor without actual orange juice.

1 medium egg

2 ounces (60 ml) Nardini amaro

¾ ounce (22.5 ml) Demerara Syrup (page 242)

2 orange peels, including 1 for garnish

Place the egg in a shaker tin without ice and dry-shake for 30 seconds. Add the amaro, Demerara syrup, and 1 of the orange peels, fill with ice, then shake until chilled. Strain into a chilled double old-fashioned glass, express and mount the remaining orange peel, and serve.

KODAK MOMENT

LIZ KELLEY

This drink is so good and one of our top sellers whenever it's on the menu. Here, Liz takes a really interesting approach to a whiskey sour—a drink that can be a little bit hardy, but here is refreshing and summery. Because the drink is made with rye, it is spicy, but then Liz brightens it up with aquavit and the amazing summer fruit notes of Amaro Pasubio, a light, wine-based blueberry amaro that also shows up in the Calvino's Cup (page 216).

½ ounce (15 ml) fresh lemon juice

¼ ounce (7.5 ml) egg white

1 ounce (30 ml) Woodford Reserve rye whiskey

¾ ounce Cappelletti Pasubio vino amaro

½ ounce (15 ml) Svol aquavit

¼ ounce (7.5 ml) Demerara Syrup (page 242)

Lemon peel

Combine the lemon juice and egg white in a shaker tin without ice and dry-shake for 30 seconds. Add the rye, amaro, aquavit, and Demerara syrup to the shaker tin, fill the shaker with ice, and shake until chilled. Double-strain into a double old-fashioned glass over 1 large ice cube. Express the lemon peel over the drink, discard it, and serve.

Flips and Fizzes

STATE STREET COCKTAIL

This is a Stanley Clisby Arthur drink that he says his wife first encountered in Mexico, where it was made with tequila. So he made his own New Orleans version with gin, and it ended up being a real crowd-pleaser. The original calls for pineapple juice, but as anyone who has ever worked with me knows, I am not a big fan of pineapple. When we developed this drink for Dauphine's, we decided to sub in a pineapple syrup, which allows us to better control the acid, sweetness, and consistency. The result is a nicely textured gin sour with juniper, lemon, lime, and mint balancing the pineapple.

½ ounce (15 ml) fresh lime juice

½ ounce (15 ml) fresh lemon juice

1 medium egg white

2 ounces (60 ml) Tanqueray gin

*1 ounce (30 ml) Pineapple Syrup
(recipe follows)*

1 spritz Peychaud's bitters

Mint sprig, for garnish

Combine the lime and lemon juice and egg white in a shaker tin without ice and dry-shake for 30 seconds. Add the gin and pineapple syrup, fill the shaker with ice, and shake until chilled. Double-strain into an old-fashioned glass filled with ice, spritz the Peychaud's from an atomizer over the surface of the drink, garnish with the mint sprig, and serve.

Pineapple Syrup

1 part fresh pineapple juice

1 part white sugar

Combine the pineapple juice and sugar in a small saucepan and bring to a boil. At the first crack of a boil, remove from the heat and continue stirring until dissolved. Allow to cool, then transfer to a nonreactive container. Store airtight in the refrigerator for up to 2 weeks.

THE GREEN FAIRY IN THE CRESCENT CITY

You've probably heard the stories: It made Van Gogh go insane and cut his ear off, it's hallucinogenic, it's illegal (or should be). Poor absinthe has been blamed for an awful lot over the years. But the truth is, it's just a spirit like any other—albeit one with a lot of cultural baggage.

Absinthe is a neutral spirit flavored with aniseed and a species of wormwood called *Artemisia absinthium*. That wormwood is where the spirit gets its name—and the source of much of the controversy, as wormwood (or more specifically, a compound it contains called thujone) was thought to be dangerous for much of the twentieth century. The truth is, thujone is lethal in very high concentrations, but as thujone is resistant to distillation, it is effectively impossible to create an absinthe with anything close to that level of toxicity.

Wormwood has been in medicinal use since the time of the ancient Egyptians, and the combination of wormwood plus aniseed was commonly used as a medicinal tonic across Europe since at least the 1600s. But absinthe *really* took off in France and Switzerland in the 1800s, especially among French troops during the colonization of Algeria in the 1840s. When the soldiers returned from North Africa to the cafés of France, they brought absinthe with them—and absinthe developed its dual reputation: as a symbol of French patrimony/fashionable accessory to bohemian café culture, and as a dangerous substance that was corrupting the country.

By the mid-1800s, absinthe's popularity had spread across Europe and into America. It found easy purchase in New Orleans, a former French colony with plenty of people with French family ties who were always looking for products that made them feel closer to home. In the latter half of the century, absinthe had become such a hot item that one of the city's most popular French Quarter bars rechristened itself the "Old Absinthe Room" or "Old Absinthe House." (That bar is still around today, and, having opened in 1806, is said to be the oldest in New Orleans.) Coffeehouses installed ornate absinthe fountains, which slowly dripped water into glasses of absinthe, properly diluting it for service. Absinthe found its way into all sorts of cocktails and even restaurant dishes, for example Antoine's Oysters Rockefeller.

Unfortunately, New Orleans didn't just import absinthe from France—it imported absinthe hysteria, too. In 1912, absinthe was banned in the United States, seven years before total Prohibition. It remained illegal for ninety-five years, until 2007, when a group led by absinthe evangelist Ted Breaux convinced the country that absinthe was not only safe, it was part of our cultural history.

When absinthe was banned, enterprising New Orleanians manufactured plenty of delicious substitutes, most famously Herbsaint, which is an anise-flavored liqueur minus the wormwood. I love Herbsaint, and we use it in plenty of cocktails here at Cure, but these days, I'm pretty thrilled to have access to the wider world of absinthe. Vieux Pontarlier is our go-to French brand, and Ted Breaux's company Jade Liqueurs makes several beautiful absinthes modeled on historical formulas from the nineteenth century. My feeling is that anyone looking to mix New Orleans–style cocktails at home should have a bottle of Herbsaint and a bottle of real-deal absinthe on their backbar at all times.

ABSINTHE SUISSESSE

This is one of my all-time favorite absinthe drinks. The first time I had an Absinthe Suissesse, it was a total revelation: It was rich and creamy and far more pleasing than I'd expect from a drink with an absinthe base. There's a reason you don't find many cocktails with a full measure of absinthe in them: Absinthe is intense and very bracing. But this preparation tones down all the more polarizing flavors of the absinthe, resulting in this luscious drink that tastes almost like an anisey eggnog.

I always think of this as a breakfast drink, but that might be because we used to make a round of Absinthe Suissesses for the team of my bar Bellocq on Mardi Gras morning. We were right on the parade route, and there was just something about sipping this on a chilly February or March morning, watching all the crowds go by. It's the ideal way to lay down a foundation for the rest of your Mardi Gras day.

1 medium egg white

1½ ounces (45 ml) Vieux Pontarlier absinthe

1 ounce (30 ml) heavy cream

¾ ounce (22.5 ml) Simple Syrup (page 243)

¼ ounce (7.5 ml) Tempus Fugit crème de menthe

Freshly grated nutmeg, for garnish

Place the egg white in a shaker tin and dry-shake vigorously for about 30 seconds to foam the egg. Add the absinthe, cream, and simple syrup, fill the shaker with ice, and shake until chilled. Double-strain into a chilled cocktail class and float the crème de menthe on top. Garnish with the nutmeg and serve.

L. KASIMU HARRIS on Preserving New Orleans's Historic Black Bars

L. Kasimu Harris is a New Orleans–born writer and photographer who also worked the door at Cure for several years. In 2018, Kasimu began work on a photo and interview project titled "Vanishing Black Bars and Lounges." His focus was a specific part of St. Bernard Avenue between Claiborne Avenue and North Rampart Street, in the heart of the Seventh Ward, a historically Black neighborhood. Gentrification and the closure of Black-owned businesses is a problem that is not limited to the Seventh Ward—it is happening across the city, and it is not lost on me that Freret, Cure's neighborhood, was predominantly Black until Hurricane Katrina forced many Black-owned businesses to close or move elsewhere. But Kasimu had grown up in the Seventh Ward, and he had a personal connection to the bars and venues on St. Bernard Avenue. He knew how much the neighborhood had changed since he was a kid and saw how quickly the number of Black-owned bars was dwindling. So he set out with his camera to capture this moment of transition, when so many Black spaces were becoming white, and to document what remained.

What is your personal connection to some of the Black bars in New Orleans?

I come from a musical family. Growing up, there was a bar called the Winner's Circle, which is now Seal's Class Act Bar on St. Bernard Avenue. My sister, Rahssana Ison, is a vocalist and seven years older than I am. The first time I remember going to a Black bar was with my mom to hear her; she used to sit in with her dad, who played with the Richwell Ison/Kirk Ford Experience. I must have been ten or eleven.

A few years later, I had another memorable moment at a bar called Little People's Place, which is still there [on Barracks Street in the Treme]. I was probably seventeen, and an aspiring trumpet player. It was Jazz Fest time, and after performing at Jazz Fest, many of the musicians would go to smaller venues to play a jam session. So at Little People's Place, you had Wynton Marsalis, Kermit Ruffins, Irvin Mayfield, and a bunch of people from the Charles Mingus Big Band. Little People's Place is small—about as big as my studio. I just remember sitting there and playing my trumpet—I had only been playing trumpet about two years, so I wasn't killing. Wynton Marsalis plays with these Monet trumpets, which are very, very well-crafted and very heavy. After a while it just gets too heavy for him to hold. So eventually he asked to play *my* trumpet. I of course gave it to him. The bandstand was right by the audience, and I remember a guy pulled me to the side: "Hey man, I bet you never heard your horn sound like that before!"

What inspired you to start your "Vanishing Black Bars and Lounges" project?

There's a stretch of land, a few blocks on St. Bernard Avenue between Claiborne and Rampart, that when I was coming up had six or seven Black bars. But when I'd talk to people a few generations older than me, they'd say there used to be *ten* Black bars on that street, and some nights, it was so crowded with people you could barely walk. It looked like a block party, with people going from bar to bar.

By 2018, those six or seven bars had turned into only one. The demographics on St. Bernard Avenue had started to change: You'd see hipsters riding bikes, white people walking through the neighborhood. A bar that I used to go to called Next Stop turned into this place called the Goat. I went in and it was totally devoid of any of its past history. They painted the bar black and gray, but it was devoid of Blackness. When the opportunity came for me to photograph these places for *Pop-Up Magazine*, I took it. I'm not an investigative journalist, and I wasn't trying to indict anyone, but I feel that if you are bold enough to move into this neighborhood and take over these Black bars, you should be able to answer questions like, "What made you move here?"

People talk about the "Bourdain effect": Anthony Bourdain would go to a place and all of a sudden a really beautiful, small place would just get blown out by tourists. Are you worried about that?

I've thought about that. It has happened in some places, like the famous juke joint in Mississippi, Po' Monkeys. Many people were first made aware of it through Birney Imes's book [*Juke Joint*, published in 1990 by the University of Mississippi Press], which was an inspiration for my project. In the 1980s, these juke joints were ubiquitous, but when I went to grad school at the University of Mississippi, they were languishing in the single digits, even though they had the exposure.

One thing about Imes is he was a white dude going into all these Black spaces. I always say that when it comes to New Orleans, I have the fascination of an outsider, but the knowledge of an insider. So when I think about it— *Could these places change [because I'm writing about them]?*—I think about the example of Willie Mae's Scotch House. As a teenager, I would go there—I remember going there with Delfeayo Marsalis—and it was just a neighborhood spot. Katrina shut it down, and the Southern Foodways Alliance helped rebuild it. Then they were acknowledged by the James Beard Foundation as one of "America's Classics," and now they've grown to have a second location.

I went to school with Kerry Seaton Stewart [Willie Mae's great-granddaughter]. And while she may be nostalgic for how it used to be, I know she doesn't mind that increased revenue!

That's the thing: You may not have some of the magic that it used to have, but what it's done for the family and the community to have that much economic activity is worth acknowledging.

Right. When I talked to Linda Green [a local food vendor who sells Yak-a-Mein, a meaty noodle soup], she said the reason some of these Black bars shuttered is because a lot of Black people who have done what you might consider back-breaking work—butchers, master carpenters, brick masons, or even bar owners—when they do well for themselves, oftentimes, not always, they don't want their kids doing that kind of work.

I talked to Victor Dawkins, who owns the Other Place, one of the last Black bars on St. Bernard Avenue. I asked him how he felt now that all the bars around him had changed.

He said, "Man, you know, I can't blame them." People gave these bar owners a good price and they took it. He said, "I've been selling the same drinks to the same people for thirty years. If somebody offers me a good price, I'm selling, too." He in particular is very adamant about not passing the torch of that bar to someone in his family. He's in his bar pulling sixteen-hour days.

I get it. As a side note, my daughter recently said, "Daddy, I think that one day, I want to own a restaurant." And I was like, "No, you don't." It's easy for us to romanticize the work that other people have dedicated their lives to.

What I wish was that New Orleans recognized the gem they have in these Black bars and realized that they are part of the cultural fabric of the city. Black culture *is* New Orleans culture. And the city could make it easier for people to reopen a bar. If a liquor license isn't active for six months, it lapses. Even during the COVID pandemic, you'd hear that people's taxes were still due; the electricity bills were still due. The City Council was shoving down all these amendments that would negatively impact bars, and I remember looking at [the legislation] and thinking, you need a lawyer to wade through this shit. There were just no accommodations.

Contrast that with the historic pubs of London. There, if you want to sell, someone can't just buy it and turn it into a massage parlor. It has to remain a bar. There they recognize the gems that they have and preserve them.

The first thing that has to happen is to acknowledge what is happening, and I think you're the first person to really address this. People have talked about disappearing Black businesses, but bars get left out of the conversation, because the cultural value of bars is always going to be cheapened.

No one thought enough of these Black bars to document them. I would Google bars that I remembered from my past, and I couldn't find records of them unless they had a longtime owner with a big personality—you might find that in an obit. Restaurants get written about; they are forever in a recorded history. But that hasn't happened for bars.

Yet in New Orleans, so much of culture, so much of our history, has happened in bars. Like places that sell food, or music venues, these are gathering spots, but we as a society never think about bars the same way. So thank you for doing this work!

ESSENTIAL NEW ORLEANS BLACK BARS AND RESTAURANTS

LITTLE PEOPLE'S PLACE. Great food and drinks at this tiny Treme spot, which has been family-run since the 1950s.

....

MOTHER-IN-LAW LOUNGE. Originally opened by Ernie K-Doe in the 1990s, Mother-in-Law is now run by trumpeter Kermit Ruffins. There's live music nearly every night, and famous muscians often drop in.

....

THE OTHER PLACE. Currently the last of the Black-owned bars on St. Bernard Avenue.

....

SPORTSMAN'S CORNER. A neighborhood spot at Second Street and Dryades run by the Elloie family.

....

DOOKY CHASE. Founded by the legendary Leah Chase, who passed in 2019, the world-famous Dooky Chase restaurant has served celebrities and leaders from Duke Ellington to Beyoncé to Barack Obama since its opening in the 1940s. The Chase family continues the tradition of serving some of the city's best Creole cooking.

....

WILLIE MAE'S SCOTCH HOUSE. Opened in 1957, Willie Mae's has been a fixture in the Fifth Ward, near the Treme, for decades. Today, Willie Mae's great-granddaughter runs the restaurant. If you don't order the legendary fried chicken, you need to reevaluate your life choices.

HIGHBALLS AND 75s

Sparkling Drinks

GUNSHOP FIZZ
(PAGE 201)

I'm definitely partial to the 75 format, which is essentially a small sour with sparkling wine on top. A collins, which is a precursor to the 75, is a small sour with soda water on top. Both are such crowd-pleasers.

There's a reason seltzer and soda manufacturers like La Croix and Coca-Cola do the kind of business they do. And there's a reason why prehistoric humans went to the trouble of converting vegetables and grains into bubbling ferments like beer. We're drawn to the sensation of liquid dancing around in our mouths. I will not speculate as to the evolutionary reasons why this is the case—I'm sure some beverage scientist has done the research—but it means that whenever I'm trying to come up with a cocktail that is sure to satisfy as many people as possible, I lean on the 75. It helps that this format is particularly well-suited to punches—the drinks in this chapter scale up nicely.

A few words of wisdom when you approach the recipes in this chapter: Make sure the source of your carbonation, whether it's sparkling wine, soda, or seltzer water, is freshly opened, with nice, tight bubbles. This may sound obvious, but I've seen too many people try to make a sparkling cocktail with flat wine or soda. In the early days of Cure, we used soda siphons to make seltzer for our cocktails. But we eventually realized that they're a pain to clean, and we weren't happy with the quality of the bubbles, so we switched to small bottles of club soda, which we open fresh for each cocktail. This is a great option for consistent bubbles at home, too. And make sure the carbonated element stays as cold as possible—don't use room-temp soda. A cold environment is essential to retain the carbonation.

FRENCH 75

The French 75 always makes it onto lists of New Orleans classic cocktails, but the truth is, it wasn't invented here, and it really didn't have much of a connection to the city until recently, in 2003. That's when the family of my friend Katy Casbarian (see page 191) rechristened the bar at their legendary French Quarter restaurant Arnaud's as Arnaud's French 75 Bar. Some say the French 75 was the favorite drink of Arnaud Cazenave, the self-proclaimed Count Arnaud who opened the restaurant in 1918. That's three years after the first known print appearance of the French 75 in a newspaper called the *Washington Herald*, so if it's true, the count was an early adopter of the cocktail.

One of the biggest modern-day cheerleaders for the French 75 is Chris Hannah, the opening bartender at Arnaud's French 75 Bar. Chris has since moved on to open his own restaurant, Jewel of the South, but in his time at the French 75 Bar he probably served up more French 75s and educated more people about the drink than anyone else in history.

One of the reasons the Casbarians and Chris made waves—besides running a fantastic bar—is they were firm believers that the drink should be made with cognac, not gin, which was more common at the time. Of course, this move sparked tons of debate and argument from nerds who love to yell at each other about how drinks should be made. As is so often the case, the historical record is pretty muddy. That first known print appearance, from 1915, states that the drink is made with gin, applejack (apple brandy), grenadine, and lemon. In 1922, the 75 Cocktail appeared in Robert Vermeire's *Cocktails: How to Mix Them* and Harry McElhone's *Harry's ABC of Mixing Cocktails*, where the recipes called for gin, Calvados (apple brandy), grenadine, and lemon (Vermeire) or no lemon (McElhone). But the most ubiquitous recipe, and the one that most modern bartenders quote, is Judge Jr.'s 1927 recipe from *Here's How!*, which calls for gin, lemon juice, sugar, and Champagne. At most bars outside of New Orleans, this is the version you'll be served when you order a French 75.

But in New Orleans, the French 75 Bar started a little brandy revolution, and now more and more people make the drink this way. At Cure, we always serve our French 75s with brandy unless a guest specifically requests gin. To me, Chris and Katy really got it right: The cocktail is good with gin, but it's *very* good with a barrel-aged spirit like brandy, which has enough weight to counterbalance the acidity and texture of the sparkling wine. To me, the French 75 is all about mouthfeel. When you make it with an unaged gin, the drink is light and zippy but sometimes a bit astringent—all you get is acid. With brandy, the warmth and texture that come from barrel aging offer some mid-notes, which in a way actually activates the bubbles in the Champagne and makes the whole drinking experience more interesting.

Another reason I like to use brandy in my French 75s is that it's a very New Orleans thing to do. Historically, New Orleanians drank a lot of brandy, at least until phylloxera screwed up the brandy trade in the late 1800s. And as David Wondrich points out, there were many punches and cups made from Champagne, lemon, sugar, and either gin (sometimes called a Champagne Cup) or brandy (a King's Peg) throughout the nineteenth century. I'm willing to bet money that New Orleanians were drinking punches made from their beloved brandy, Champagne, and lemon throughout the eighteenth century, well before World War I and the invention of the machine gun from which the French 75 cocktail gets its name.

Cocktail history has a lot of moments akin to Columbus showing up in the Caribbean and declaring that he'd discovered the New World. Whoever popularized the French 75 surely didn't come up with the idea of combining a spirit, Champagne, sugar, and lemon; they just converted it from a punch to a single-serve and gave the drink a marketable name. During World War I and the years immediately following, grape brandy would have been harder to come by than gin because of phylloxera; this explains why all those early recipes relied on some combo of gin and apple brandy. But the choice to serve the drink with grape brandy has historical precedent, too: It's a descendent of the brandy-Champagne punches that were popular in the 1800s, even if they weren't called French 75s. To me, using brandy just feels like the New Orleans thing to do—and you know how we New Orleanians love to put our own spin on things.

1½ ounces (45 ml) Sainte Louise brandy

½ ounce (15 ml) fresh lemon juice

½ ounce (15 ml) Simple Syrup (page 243)

Sparkling wine (see Note), to top

Lemon peel, for garnish

Combine the brandy, lemon juice, and simple syrup in a cocktail shaker filled with ice and short-shake (about ten shakes) so as not to overdilute. Double-strain into a cocktail glass and top with sparkling wine. Express and mount the lemon peel and serve.

Note: At Arnaud's French 75 Bar, you'll find that all their French 75s are made with Champagne—i.e., real-deal, AOC-protected sparkling wine from the Champagne region of France. While this is certainly an aesthetically and historically understandable choice, it starts to get pretty pricey. Because of its cachet, Champagne tends to be substantially more expensive than comparable sparkling wines made in other regions. At Cure, we use a high-quality *crémant* wine—a sparkling wine made using a similar process as Champagne but in other regions of France, for example the Loire Valley (*crémant de Loire*) or the Jura (*crémant du Jura*). At home, go to a reputable independent wine shop and ask the staff to help you pick out a good-quality sparkler ($15 is the minimum you're likely to spend) that isn't too sweet and will work well in cocktails. You can also use cava or prosecco, as long as it's good!

KATY CASBARIAN on French 75s
and Maintaining a Legacy

Katy Casbarian is the co-owner and operator (along with her mom, Jane, and brother, Archie) of Arnaud's restaurant in the heart of the French Quarter. She also happens to be a former school-mate of mine and is like a sister to me. As soon as I started writing this book, I knew I wanted to talk to Katy, because her family pretty much single-handedly catapulted the French 75 to inter-national stardom. They didn't invent the drink—it had been around for decades by the time the Casbarians opened the French 75 Bar—but if they hadn't decided to make it the centerpiece of their bar, I really do think the 75 would have remained a historical curiosity. Today, it is consid-ered a core part of the New Orleans cocktail canon. Only a handful of contemporary restaurant operators can say they've shaped the city's culinary landscape in such a major way.

How did you guys decide to open the French 75 Bar?

A little backstory: The restaurant Arnaud's was founded in 1918 by a gentleman named Arnaud Cazenave. In the beginning, the restaurant was just the area we now refer to as the main dining room. As the restaurant grew in popularity, Arnaud would buy adjacent buildings, knock a hole in a wall, and essen-tially expand the dining room. So it became a sort of labyrinth of different dining rooms, expanding across a number of buildings, which my family expanded even further.

Arnaud ran the restaurant for thirty years. He left it to his daughter, who ran it for thirty years more. She sold it to my parents at the end of the seventies. She didn't have any heirs who were of age at the time, so she had to look outside of the family to sell. My father ran a number of hotel properties in the region and was always interested in the food and bever-age side of hotel operations. They had formed a relationship, and she actually approached him about purchasing the restaurant.

When my parents bought the restaurant, restoring it was quite an undertaking, because the restaurant had fallen on hard times. Pretty quickly they realized they needed an additional bar to service the restaurant. It had a number of service bars, but it didn't have enough stand-alone or stand-in bars.

What is now the French 75 Bar used to be an all-male dining room. My parents decided to turn it into a bar, which they called the Grill Bar because it was originally the Men's Grill Room.

They wanted to create a bar that looked like what it would've looked like when the restaurant opened in 1918. So they asked an antiques dealer to bring in an antique back-bar and other authentic period details. By the early 2000s, my parents decided to rename the bar. They knew they wanted to name it after a cocktail and in particular, a French-sounding cocktail. The idea was that the bar would feel like a little oasis on Bourbon Street, so when you walked in, you felt like you'd stepped back in time, but into France.

The French 75 doesn't necessarily have anything to do with France, apart from the name. Some say it was the favorite drink of Count Arnaud (who was French), but I think some creative liberties have been taken there. It sounds good to me, but who knows? I will say

this: My father, who is now deceased, was an *avid* cognac drinker. I mean, he drank probably a half a bottle of cognac a night. So while we do feel that the proper way to make a French 75 is with cognac, we also feel it's a very fitting tribute to my dad to make them this way. For me, our choice to use cognac is a little bit more about my dad than Count Arnaud.

My parents had dialed in the recipe we were going to use before we ever opened the French 75 Bar. It was always cognac. When [the opening bartender] Chris Hannah came along, the recipe was tweaked a little bit, but the concept stayed the same. They were very intentional. Every restaurant and bar wants to have one thing, if not more, that they're really well-known for. It could be a dessert or a main dish or a flaming drink. Credit to my parents—they hit the nail on the head with their French 75.

How does it feel to operate a restaurant like Arnaud's where so many classic New Orleans dishes, like Shrimp Arnaud and Oysters Bienville, were invented? Do you feel a responsibility to preserve them?

Everyone who has worked in this industry knows that consistency is one of the hardest marks to hit. You have to build the right team, and they need to hit the mark every day.

People come in and expect to have a dish exactly the same way they had it the day before. Credit to chefs who are creative and reinventing their menus constantly, but it's equally impressive, if not more so, when a chef can handle the pressure of delivering the same perfect dish every day and living up to their guests' expectations of what a historic dish is supposed to taste like.

We consider ourselves stewards, keepers of tradition. And I feel like New Orleans is one of the few cities that really values history and tradition. Sometimes when I talk to the press, they want to know, "What's the hot new thing? What are you doing that's pushing the envelope?" The best answer I can give is we're coming in every day and being super consistent on a one hundred-year-old recipe.

What's your favorite cocktail?

This is totally cliché, and I feel like I'm going to be shamed for my answer, but the French 75 is my favorite cocktail! They taste delicious, obviously, but it's also a drink that makes me nostalgic for my family. And so it's not just the taste. I also love a gimlet.

Would the Cazenave family appreciate Arnaud's if they walked in today?

I think they would be pleased. I mean, we honor them—their legacy and the dishes that they created—every day.

We've been able to expand our reach and our audience without deviating from who we truly are. We are true to our roots. That doesn't mean that we haven't done some different stuff here; we've had crazy themed events like a Beyoncé Brunch, to honor her birthday, with drag queens and all of her best music. But it seemed like Count Arnaud and the Cazenaves liked to have a good time, so who knows? Maybe they would have liked it!

HOWITZER

HOWITZER

NEAL BODENHEIMER

This may seem hard to believe today, given the popularity of Southern food. But in the early 2000s, Southern cooks and drink-makers were still trying to convince the rest of the country that the South is culturally relevant. That's what was in my head when I started working on the Howitzer. It was the first original to be featured on a Cure menu.

My idea was to pair two of the most Southern ingredients out there: bourbon and peaches. The French 75 was already a popular template in New Orleans, and there was much debate as to whether it should be made with gin or cognac, so using bourbon as a base seemed to me like a funny way to bypass that conversation entirely. The French 75 was named after a big-ass French gun, so I decided to name my drink after a big-ass American gun.

1½ ounces (45 ml) Evan Williams single-barrel whiskey

½ ounce (15 ml) Simple Syrup (page 243)

½ ounce (15 ml) fresh lemon juice

7 drops Fee Brothers peach bitters

Sparkling wine, to top

Lemon peel, for garnish

Combine all the ingredients except the sparkling wine and lemon peel in a shaker filled with ice. Shake until chilled and double-strain into a cocktail glass. Top with the sparkling wine, express and mount the lemon peel, and serve.

MISS CAMILLE

KIRK ESTOPINAL

This French 75 riff is really just a vehicle for a specific product Kirk was excited about, Marolo Milla's chamomile liqueur. Sometimes drink creation is as simple as that: You see a bottle you're excited to try, and then you play around until you find a template that shows it off well. When this first went on the menu, a couple came in and excitedly ordered it because their daughter is named Camille. Years later, that same Camille became my daughter, Hayden's, first nanny. When her parents come in, I'm always so excited to see them and to serve them a Miss Camille.

1½ ounces (45 ml) Evan Williams single-barrel whiskey

1 ounce (30 ml) Marolo Milla grappa and chamomile liqueur

¾ ounce (22.5 ml) fresh lemon juice

¼ ounce (7.5 ml) Honey Syrup (page 243)

Sparkling wine, to top

Lemon peel, for garnish

Combine all the ingredients except the sparkling wine and garnish in a shaker filled with ice. Shake until chilled and double-strain into a cocktail glass. Top with the sparkling wine, express and mount the lemon peel, and serve.

Highballs and 75s

CELERY STALKER

DANNY VALDÉZ

This is a cocktail that I've noticed popping up on other bars' menus around the country, which is how you know it's really good. Danny has such a talent for making straightforward drinks that are nevertheless total bangers. His Chamomile Kilt (page 138) is another example of this. The Celery Stalker is a simple concept: a sparkling cucumber gimlet with lime instead of lemon (since cucumber and lime are such a killer pairing) and celery bitters to make it savory and pull it into the vegetal 75 category. It remains incredibly popular and is one of the Cure originals we serve at our location in the New Orleans airport.

Combine all the ingredients except the sparkling wine and cucumber in a shaker filled with ice. Shake until chilled, then double-strain into a chilled cocktail glass. Top with the sparkling wine, garnish with the cucumber slice, and serve.

1 ounce (30 ml) Beefeater gin

½ ounce (15 ml) fresh lime juice

½ ounce (15 ml) Simple Syrup (page 243)

10 drops Bitter Truth celery bitters

Sparkling wine, to top

Cucumber slice, for garnish

JETS TO BRAZIL

CHRISTINA RANDO

Melons, especially honeydews and cantaloupes, are quite difficult to use in cocktails because of their high water content. When you try to use whole fruit, they tend to thin out and lose their essence. Christina made the smart choice of turning the cantaloupe into a syrup, so you can really concentrate that melon flavor. The cachaça she uses has these great cinnamon and bison grass notes (which I think of as vegetal and cinnamony but less earthy than cinnamon proper), which she pairs with Aperol, since Aperol and cinnamon go so well together. The result is a really lovely 75-style sour that was very popular as soon as it hit the menu.

1 ounce (30 ml) Avuá Amburana cachaça

¾ ounce (22.5 ml) Aperol

¼ ounce (7.5 ml) St-Germain elderflower liqueur

1 ounce (30 ml) fresh lemon juice

½ ounce (15 ml) Cantaloupe Syrup (recipe follows)

7 drops Peychaud's bitters

½ ounce (15 ml) soda water, to top

Combine all the ingredients except the soda water in a shaker filled with ice. Shake until chilled, then double-strain into a chilled cocktail glass. Top with the soda water and serve.

Cantaloupe Syrup

MAKES ABOUT 1½ CUPS (360 ML)

½ cantaloupe (about 1½ pounds / 680 g), peeled, cored, and cut into cubes

White sugar

In a blender, puree the cantaloupe until smooth, then fine-strain. Combine the strained juice with an equal part of white sugar in the blender, then blend on medium speed for about 5 minutes. Store airtight in the refrigerator for up to 3 days.

ROFFIGNAC

The Roffignac made its first book appearance in our guy Stanley Clisby Arthur's *Famous New Orleans Drinks and How to Mix 'Em*. This one is definitely a regional specialty, not very well known outside of New Orleans. It was named after the tenth mayor of the city, Count Louis Philippe Joseph de Roffignac. Most historians say Joe was an effective mayor; he oversaw the paving of Royal Street and the installation of the city's first street lights. Although he was purportedly a bon vivant, he didn't invent his namesake cocktail and probably never tasted one, since he died in 1846 and the drink doesn't show up in print until much later.

Stanley Clisby Arthur's Roffignac recipe is an odd one because of its inclusion of a mystery ingredient, "Hembarig," which confused booze nerds for many years. Arthur writes that it was "a popular sirup when old New Orleans was young," and he suggests subbing raspberry syrup or grenadine. But Southern culinary historian Robert Moss has a slightly more detailed accounting.

"Arthur, it turns out, was working phonetically," Moss writes in *Southern Spirits*, "and what he heard as 'red hembarig' was actually 'red himbeeressig,' a syrup whose name combines the German word for raspberries (*Himbeer*) with the German word for vinegar (*Essig*)."

Now we have liftoff. If you drink a Roffignac that is made with the raspberry syrup or grenadine Arthur calls for, you get a flabby, too-sweet whiskey soda that is just begging for acid. Sub in a raspberry shrub, and suddenly the drink makes sense.

It's worth noting that Arthur's recipe calls for whiskey, but I straight-up do not like a whiskey Roffignac, and the original recipe as popularized at Mannessier's Confectionery was almost certainly made with brandy. That said, the Roffig-nac works surprisingly well with any number of unaged spirits. At Peychaud's, we use Cobra Fire, an unaged Armagnac blanche, and it is so, so good. At Dauphine's, we take even more creative license and offer a tequila Roffignac. You could try it with gin or even vodka.

1½ ounces (45 ml) Darroze 8 Year "Les Grands Assemblages" Bas-Armagnac

1 ounce (30 ml) Raspberry Shrub (recipe follows)

Soda water, to top

Fresh raspberries, for garnish

Combine the Armagnac and shrub in a cocktail shaker filled with ice and shake until chilled. Double-strain into a collins glass filled with ice and top with the soda water. Garnish with the fresh raspberries and serve.

Raspberry Shrub

MAKES ABOUT 2½ CUPS (600 ML)

1 cup (125 g) fresh raspberries

1 cup (240 ml) cold water

1 cup (200 g) white sugar

1 cup (240 ml) white vinegar

Combine all the ingredients in the bowl of a food processor or blender and puree. Strain through a fine-mesh sieve into a nonreactive container. Store airtight in the refrigerator for up to 3 months.

MARIO PUZO

KIRK ESTOPINAL

"There's a classic old drink called The Godfather that's a duo of Scotch and amaretto," Kirk says. "It's a cool flavor combination, but those two ingredients alone together in a glass are pretty fucking gross." So Kirk set out to improve the classic, emphasizing the smoky notes but making it more bright and refreshing with citrus and orange flower water.

2 ounces (60 ml) Springbank 100-proof
single malt Scotch

¾ ounce (22.5 ml) fresh lemon juice

½ ounce (15 ml) Lazzaroni amaretto

½ ounce (15 ml) Simple Syrup (page 243)

12 drops orange flower water

Seltzer, to top

Combine all the ingredients except the seltzer in a shaker filled with ice. Shake until chilled, then double-strain into a collins glass filled with ice. Top with seltzer and serve.

GUNSHOP FIZZ

KIRK ESTOPINAL AND MAKS PAZUNIAK

This is one of the most famous drinks on our menu. "The Gunshop Fizz was kind of the impetus for *Rogue Cocktails*," Kirk said. "We were looking around for weird old drinks, and we found an Angostura Fizz in Charles Baker's book [*The Gentleman's Companion*, from 1939]. It had a half ounce of Angostura, dry vermouth, and soda. We made it and didn't really like it, but the idea of it—to have such a large measure of bitters—was fascinating." They decided to build the drink somewhat like a Pimm's Cup, macerating the Peychaud's with fresh fruit, then building it into a sour. The Sanbitter, a bright-red, bitter soda made by San Pellegrino, can be hard to come by; in a pinch you can sub Campari mixed with soda (or just omit it). "Something I really like about this drink is the color," Kirk says. "It's the reddest thing in the world, insanely red. It flew in the face of the mixology rules of the time, because it practically looks artificial." But that's yet another thing that made it rogue.

2 ounces (60 ml) Peychaud's bitters

3 grapefruit peels

3 orange peels

2 strawberries, hulled

4 slices cucumber, including 1 for garnish

1 ounce (30 ml) fresh lemon juice

1 ounce (30 ml) Simple Syrup (page 243)

Sanbitter, for topping

Combine the Peychaud's, grapefruit peels, orange peels, strawberries, and 3 of the cucumber slices in the tin of a shaker and muddle. Allow to soak for 2 minutes, then add the lemon juice and simple syrup and shake until chilled. Double-strain into a collins glass filled with ice, top with the Sanbitter, garnish with the remaining cucumber slice, and serve.

RED MEDICINE

KIRK ESTOPINAL

Kirk describes this as a Bloody Mary he actually wants to drink. "Bloody Marys are notoriously salty, and I just don't like them very much." So when he was invited to visit the Marsh House, the facility where Tabasco makes its product, he got to thinking about an "avant-garde brunch drink." (Which is funny, because Cure doesn't serve brunch.) "I started thinking about shrubs: A shrub is fruit and vinegar, so a vinegar-and-chile hot sauce like Tabasco is, in a way, like a shrub." That inspired him to add some sugar and mix it with Pimm's, resulting in a low-proof, refreshing, *not* salty Bloody Mary for people who don't like Bloody Marys.

2 ounces (60 ml) Pimm's No. 1 Cup liqueur

¾ ounce (22.5 ml) fresh lemon juice

½ ounce (15 ml) Tabasco Shrub (recipe follows)

10 drops Bitter Truth celery bitters

Seltzer, to top

Cucumber slice, for garnish

Combine all the ingredients except the seltzer and cucumber slice in a shaker filled with ice. Shake until chilled and double-strain into a collins glass. Top with the seltzer, garnish with the cucumber slice, and serve.

Tabasco Shrub

2 parts Demerara Syrup (page 242)

1 part Tabasco hot sauce

1 part water

Combine the ingredients in a saucepan and bring to a simmer over medium-high heat. Cook for 10 minutes, then remove from the heat and transfer to a nonreactive container. Store airtight in the refrigerator for up to 4 weeks.

Highballs and 75s

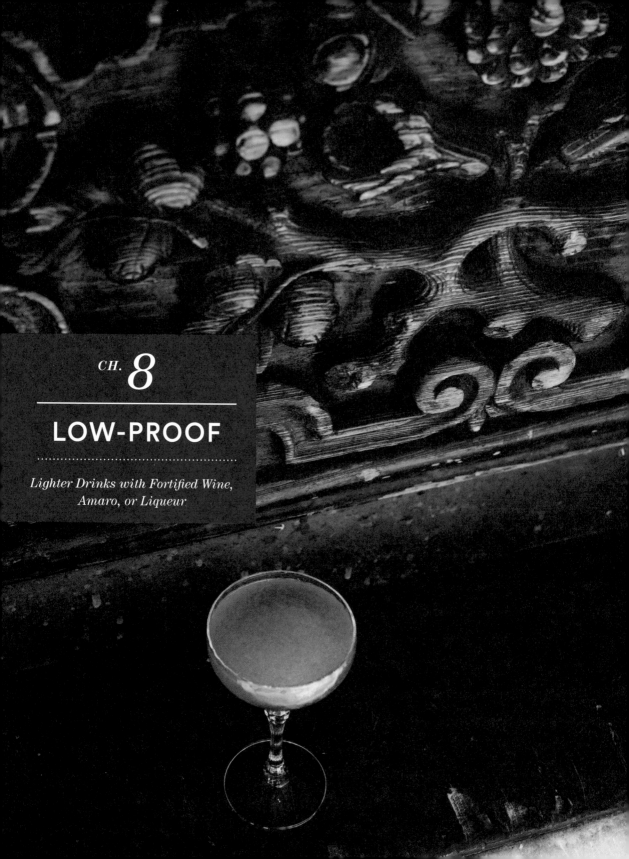

Many people today look at low-proof cocktails as something new and trendy, a flash in the pan that will go out of style in a year or two. But in reality, low-proof drinking is the oldest style of drinking there is. It took a long time for humankind to figure out how to concentrate alcohol into something high-proof. And even after distillation technology became more widespread, people were still consuming mostly beer, wine, cider, mead, and later vermouth, Madeira, and other fortified wines.

Colonial and nineteenth-century Americans famously drank a *lot*—way more than we do today. Blame the rugged frontier lifestyle or the fact that potable drinking water was a precious commodity. But the fact is, most people (unless they were early teetotalers) were half-intoxicated most of the time. Nowhere was this truer than in New Orleans, where there has always been a crazy rate of bars per capita. According to Elizabeth M. Williams and Chris McMillian in *Lift Your Spirits*, it was somewhere around one bar per sixty-six residents in 1745. To put this in context, in 2012, the real estate platform Trulia mapped out the American cities with the highest density of bars, and New Orleans topped the list . . . at 8.6 bars per *ten thousand* households.

Back in the old days, low-proof drinks were a necessity. Eventually, you needed to switch to something a bit watered down, otherwise you weren't going to get through your day. The need for lower-proof cocktails might not be quite as urgent today—there are easier and more effective ways to stay hydrated. But in many ways, the appeal of low-proof cocktails remains the same. Who doesn't want to keep the party going, to drink a little more and a little longer without feeling the ill effects of too much alcohol?

CABILDO COBBLERS

These next three recipes nod to one of my favorite stories about New Orleans's integration into the United States. Everybody learns in school that Thomas Jefferson made one of the best real estate deals in American history when he purchased the Louisiana Territory from France. But the French had been in control of the region for only a short time prior to the purchase; from 1763 to 1802, it was controlled by the Spanish. So really, the Louisiana Purchase was a three-way affair between the Spanish, who officially conveyed the land to France on November 30, 1803; the French, who turned it over to the United States three weeks later; and us.

It's probably apocryphal, but legend has it that when representatives from Spain, France, and the United States dined at the Spanish colonial city hall in New Orleans, the Cabildo, to commemorate the deal, they had three separate toasts: sherry, a product of Spain; brandy, from France; and Madeira, a favorite among the American colonial elite.

Cognac Cobbler

....

2 lemon quarter-wheels

1½ ounces (45 ml) Pierre Ferrand 1840 cognac

1½ ounces (45 ml) Pierre Ferrand pineau des Charantes

½ ounce (15 ml) fresh lemon juice

2 barspoons superfine sugar

14 drops Bittermens Boston Bittahs

2 raspberries, for garnish

Mint sprig, for garnish

Madeira Cobbler

....

2 lemon quarter-wheels

3 ounces (90 ml) Rare Wine Co. Charleston Sercial Madeira

½ ounce (15 ml) Simple Syrup (page 243)

1 blueberry, for garnish

1 strawberry slice, for garnish

Mint sprig, for garnish

Sherry Cobbler

....

2 lemon quarter-wheels

2 orange quarter-wheels

2½ ounces (75 ml) Oloroso sherry

½ ounce (15 ml) Simple Syrup (page 243)

Orange peel, for garnish

Strawberry slice, for garnish

Mint sprig, for garnish

Muddle the citrus quarter-wheels in a shaker tin, then add the remaining ingredients except the garnish and fill the shaker with ice. Shake until chilled, then double-strain into a cobbler tin or double old-fashioned glass filled with crushed ice. Garnish with the fresh fruit, mint, and citrus (if using), then serve.

KING'S COBBLER

NEAL BODENHEIMER

There is something magical about the combination of Zucca and strawberry. Rhubarb and
strawberry is one of the all-time great dessert
pairings, and it turns out the rhubarb in the amaro
works really well with strawberry, too. So I kept
it simple for this sour-style cobbler, to really let
the flavor combo shine.

½ strawberry, hulled

2 ounces (60 ml) Zucca Rabarbaro amaro

¾ ounce (22.5 ml) fresh lemon juice

¾ ounce (22.5 ml) Simple Syrup
  (page 243)

Strawberry fan, for garnish

Muddle the strawberry in a shaker tin, then
add the Zucca, lemon juice, and simple
syrup. Fill the shaker with ice, shake until
chilled, and double-strain into a double
old-fashioned glass filled with crushed ice.
Garnish with the strawberry fan and serve.

OLD HICKORY

To me, the Old Hickory is an underrated classic:
It's balanced, complex, and feels modern despite
its nineteenth-century origins. The Old Hickory
appears in Arthur's *Famous New Orleans Drinks*,
where he writes, "According to hoary but unsub-
stantiated tradition, this was the favorite tipple of
Andrew Jackson when he was in New Orleans
the winter of 1814–15 helping pirate Jean Laffite
with the Battle of New Orleans." Sadly, that story
sounds like bullshit to me—Americans weren't
really drinking vermouth until the 1850s, and the
first vermouth ad I found in any Louisiana newspaper was from 1852.

At Dauphine's, we batch the vermouths
together ahead of time and refrigerate them,
which allows us to mix the ingredients without
ice so as not to overdilute the drink. This helps
preserve the character of the vermouth.

1½ ounces (45 ml) La Quintinye Royal
  blanc vermouth

1½ ounces (45 ml) Cinzano Rosso vermouth

14 drops Peychaud's bitters

7 drops Regans' orange bitters

Lemon peel, for garnish

Combine all the ingredients except the
garnish in a mixing glass without ice and stir.
Pour into a double old-fashioned glass over
1 large ice cube, garnish with the lemon peel,
and serve.

OLD HICKORY

PABLEAUX JOHNSON on the Power of Red Beans

Pableaux Johnson is a jack-of-all-trades and master of quite a few: photographer, writer, designer, and more. He has been coming to Cure since we opened, and you can often find him at the start of service in his designated spot (the corner seat of the bar).

Over the years, Pableaux has become a bit of a local legend for his weekly red beans dinners, which he hosts at his home every Monday and which always attract a colorful crowd. I can think of few people who are as devoted to building community as Pableaux is. He really has mastered the New Orleans art form of bringing people together over good food and drink.

Talk to me about the origin of your red beans parties.

When I went to college in Austin, Texas, I would do these large-format house parties. It started as turkey-bone gumbo the Saturday after Thanksgiving and then grew into a full-day afternoon party once every three months or so, usually with gumbo and red beans. We'd open the house, and a hundred to two hundred people would show up over the course of the day.

I come from a big family within a big family and was remarkably close to my mother's father and mother's mother. We grew up around the kitchen table—specifically the kitchen table, not the dining room table. It seats about twelve, depending on how many leaves are in it; it can have fewer leaves in it but rarely does. When my grandfather passed away, they were taking apart the house and asked, "Who has room for this table?" I was just moving to New Orleans with my then-girlfriend, and it just so happened that we had a fantastic, cavernous apartment down on Magazine Street with room for the table.

That's a long way around the barn to say, I decided when I moved here that I was going to fill this table in my grandmother's honor once a week, because a table this big doesn't like it when nobody's seated there.

Instead of doing a giant blowout house party every couple of months, I said, *Every Monday, no matter what, I'm going to fill this table and cook red beans.* If I had gone in saying, *I think I'll have a dinner party once a week*, it just never would have worked. I don't necessarily believe in "dinner parties," but I do believe in getting people around the table and making it as low-stakes as possible. Whoever I'd run into that week, I'd ask, "Hey, what are you doing on Monday night?" Nobody's ever doing anything on a Monday night, especially chefs and bartenders, who tend to be off.

Everyone gets the same text: "Red Beans info: [My address], Uptown. 7:00. Casual. Bring whatchawannadrink." People ask, "Can I bring a salad?" No, you cannot bring a salad, because it will just make more work for me.

I developed my red beans over years of cooking, with things that I learned from different important people in my life—like adding dried sweet basil, which I learned from one of my old high school teachers. I use andouille and smoked sausage from La Place, one of the legendary sausage-making capitals of south Louisiana. I do it in a pressure cooker, which means I can make the first onion cut at 6:45 and have it on the table by 7:30. It's muscle memory. I use a rice cooker, so I don't have to think about that, and make skillet cornbread, which I learned from my grandfather. We have whiskey for dessert.

It turns out that a significant number of people like drinking wine on a Monday, eating decent grandma food, and having a little snort of whiskey before they go home and face the rest of the week. I've been doing it for more than twenty years now, and it has never been the same collection of people at the table twice, whether it's friends of friends or a chef visiting from out of town.

Sitting at that table has become really important to me and the community of journalists, restaurant people, and folks I know here. We came back the red-hot second we could after Katrina. It was an anchor, a way to just process stuff. We could tell stories and joke.

We have certain very simple rules that have developed over time. It's always ten to twelve people. There's no assigned seating and nothing formal. I literally throw spoons in the middle of the table. I uncork all the wine to make sure it's there if people want it and no one has to politely ask for more. I go deep grandma and say no phones at the table at all.

I played jazz in my younger days. What you learn is that so much of that particular form is freedom within structure. This is kind of an application of that. The structure is the dish, red beans, and the place, which is my family table. The rest is improvisation. It's very New Orleanian: This is a very, very generous and informal city.

What's your favorite New Orleans drinking experience?

That corner seat at the bar at Cure, at the beginning of the shift, is hands down my favorite. That's not me blowing smoke. My first drink will always be a daiquiri in a bucket, which means in a rocks glass rather than a coupe. It's my idiosyncrasy, and I always catch no end of shit from certain bartenders behind the stick there and from my drinking companions. They roll their eyes, but I don't care.

GLOBAL CITY #2

MATT YOUNG

This is a refreshing sour built on a foundation of port, inspired by the Manila Hoop Punch, an obscure classic cocktail from Charles H. Baker's 1939 book *The Gentleman's Companion.* The original calls for port, cognac, curaçao, and lemon, but Matt decided to take it in a different direction with a Czech herbal liqueur called Becherovka, which has a warm, almost baking-spice profile that also shows up in Jamaican rum and Brazilian cachaça. The result is a layered cinnamon flavor and plenty of ripe fruit from the port.

1½ ounces (45 ml) Feist tawny port

¾ ounce (22.5 ml) fresh lime juice

½ ounce (15 ml) Simple Syrup (page 243)

¼ ounce (7.5 ml) Becherovka

¼ ounce (7.5 ml) Smith and Cross
　　traditional Jamaican rum

¼ ounce (7.5 ml) Avuá Amburana cachaça

Mint sprig, for garnish

Orange peel, for garnish

Combine all the ingredients except the garnishes in a shaker tin without ice and dry-shake for 30 seconds. Double-strain into a double-old fashioned glass filled with crushed ice, garnish with the mint sprig and orange peel, and serve.

AS WINE STANDS TIME

KIRK ESTOPINAL

This is basically an inverted 2:1 Manhattan, with the Italian bitters Cynar and French Bonal subbing in for the vermouth. Kirk's rogue move here is to stir instead of shake the drink, which would be expected for a drink with fresh citrus, and to serve it in a no-frills Delmonico glass. "It's brown, it's not very pretty. And that's what I like about this drink: It goes against the idea that specific styles of drinks need to be served in specific vessels, garnished a certain way, etc. But it's a great drink! It's still got it."

¾ ounce (22.5 ml) Cynar

¾ ounce (22.5 ml) Bonal

¾ ounce (22.5 ml) Pikesville rye

¾ ounce (22.5 ml) fresh grapefruit juice

Grapefruit peel, for garnish

Combine all the ingredients except the garnish in a mixing glass filled with ice and stir until chilled. Strain into a Delmonico glass, garnish with the grapefruit peel, and serve.

Low-Proof

CADIZ BRAMBLE

DAMNED IF YOU DO

NICHOLAS JARRETT

This is Nick's take on the classic Pimm's Royale (a cocktail made with Pimm's, sparkling wine, and muddled cucumber and/or fruit), where he substitutes bright Italian amaro, complex Spanish vermouth, and a touch of French floral liqueur for the standard Pimm's No. 1. "The combination of Bittermens Burlesque bitters and Boston Bittahs with an equal part of saline solution plays particularly nicely here, and was subsequently used in a few different seasonal cocktails over the years."

1 ounce (30 ml) Amaro Montenegro

1 ounce (30 ml) Priorat Natur Vermut

1 ounce (30 ml) fresh lemon juice

½ ounce (15 ml) St-Germain elderflower liqueur

¼ ounce (7.5 ml) Simple Syrup (page 243)

15 drops BBS (see Note)

Sparkling wine, to top

Cucumber slice, for garnish

Combine all the ingredients except the sparkling wine and cucumber slice in a shaker tin filled with ice and shake until chilled. Double-strain into a collins glass filled with ice, top with sparkling wine, garnish with the cucumber slice, and serve.

Note: To make the BBS, combine equal parts Bittermens Boston Bittahs, Bittermens Burlesque bitters, and Saline Solution (page 243).

CADIZ BRAMBLE

RYAN GANNON

Cadiz Street is a couple of blocks up from Cure, but it's also a town in the Spanish Sherry Triangle, near the bodega where Fernando de Castilla is produced. If you don't know if you're a sherry fan, definitely try this drink. It's salty and briny, but also fruity and refreshing thanks to the currant notes of the cassis. It's a Mediterranean vacation in a glass. Bonus: If you want to scale this up and batch it, it works really well as a pitcher drink.

2 ounces (60 ml) Fernando de Castilla fino sherry

¾ ounce (22.5 ml) fresh lemon juice

¾ ounce (22.5 ml) Simple Syrup (page 243)

¼ ounce (7.5 ml) Clear Creek cassis liqueur, to top

Combine the sherry, lemon juice, and simple syrup in a shaker without ice and dry-shake for about 30 seconds until combined. Dump into a double old-fashioned glass filled with crushed ice, float the cassis liqueur on top, and serve.

Low-Proof

DARK PASSENGER

GENEVIEVE MASHBURN

"My favorite cocktail is a sidecar," a foundational classic with cognac, orange liqueur, and lemon, Genevieve tells me. "At Cure, I was introduced to the Nardini line of grappas and was particularly smitten with the Mandorla, which is akin to an amaretto without the cloying sweetness. This drink just came together really nicely and remains probably my favorite cocktail I've made behind the bar at Cure or anywhere else, for that matter. Also, I was watching a lot of *Dexter* at the time, and for a sidecar variation, the name fit." This is a rich, complex sour and a total winner.

1½ ounces (45 ml) Rare Wine Savannah
   Verdelho Madeira

¾ ounce (22.5 ml) Pierre Ferrand
   1840 cognac

¾ ounce (22.5 ml) fresh lemon juice

½ ounce (15 ml) Nardini Mandorla grappa

Scant ¼ ounce (7.5 ml) Demerara Syrup
   (page 242)

14 drops Amargo Vallet amaro

Lemon peel, for garnish

Combine all the ingredients except the garnish in a shaker filled with 2 large ice cubes. Shake vigorously just until chilled, then strain into a chilled cocktail glass, garnish with the lemon peel, and serve.

CALVINO'S CUP

MATT LOFINK

"This is my version of a darker, grungier Pimm's Cup," Matt tells me, referring to the classic English refresher that became a New Orleans favorite. Pasubio is a wine-based amaro with juicy blueberry notes balanced with a pine-sap earthiness. It's the star of the show here and turns the drink a beautiful color. Matt suggests dry-shaking the drink. "If you've ever tasted a good red wine with an ice cube or water in it, you know that the wine completely loses its body. The same happens with a wine-based amaro."

2 ounces (60 ml) Cappelletti Pasubio vino
   amaro

½ ounce (15 ml) fresh lemon juice

½ ounce (15 ml) Cinnamon Syrup (page
   242)

½ ounce (15 ml) green Chartreuse

2 ounces (60 ml) soda water

Lemon wheel, for garnish

Combine all the ingredients except the soda water and garnish in a shaker tin without ice and dry-shake for about 30 seconds until combined. Add the soda water to the tin, then pour the contents of the tin into a collins glass filled with ice. Garnish with the lemon wheel and serve.

CALVINO'S CUP

DEW POINT BREAK

DEW POINT BREAK

NEAL BODENHEIMER

I created this drink at the height of two major cocktail trends of the last decade or so: spritzes and Toki highballs (highballs made with Japanese whiskey). I asked myself, *What would happen if I combined the two? How could I get there?* Kina d'Or is bitter and viscous and seemed well-suited to the spritz format. I realized I needed another element to bridge the Kina and Toki together and landed on apricot, since it's an ingredient that works with each individually.

Here in New Orleans, it's not necessarily the heat that gets you, it's the humidity. On muggy summer days, you're just waiting for the dew point to break. To me, this cocktail is the liquid equivalent of that refreshing moment.

¾ ounce (22.5 ml) Tempus Fugit Kina
   l'Aéro d'Or Aperitif

¾ ounce (22.5 ml) Suntory Toki whiskey

½ teaspoon (2.5 ml) Giffard Abricot du
   Roussillon liqueur

1½ ounces (45 ml) sparkling wine, to top

1½ ounces (45 ml) soda water, to top

Grapefruit twist, for garnish

Strawberry, for garnish

Build all the ingredients except the garnishes in a wine glass filled with 3 large ice cubes. Stir until chilled, then fill the glass with cracked ice. Garnish with the grapefruit twist and strawberry and serve.

DRINK OF LAUGHTER AND FORGETTING

MICHAEL YUSKO

Michael says, "I never worked on a cocktail until there was a gun to my head," which I can confirm as accurate. "With a couple hours to lay something down—or risk being fired—I grabbed the bottle of Cynar I'd been shooting all night and went to work. I poured an ounce and a half in a tin as the base, flipped a coin that landed on lime, and added a half ounce of Demerara. I paused, knowing something was missing. At that moment, Turk handed me a shot of green Chartreuse. Without thinking too much about it, I measured out a half ounce, tossed it in the tin, and shot the rest. As soon as I strained it into a coupe, I knew in my heart it was an instant classic."

1½ ounces (45 ml) Cynar

½ ounce (15 ml) green Chartreuse

¾ ounce (22.5 ml) fresh lime juice

½ ounce (15 ml) Demerara Syrup (page
   242)

14 drops Angostura bitters, plus 1 spritz for
   garnish

Combine all the ingredients except the garnish in a shaker filled with ice. Shake until chilled, then double-strain into a chilled cocktail glass. Spritz the Angostura from an atomizer over the surface of the drink and serve.

Low-Proof

FIORE AMARO

BILLY DOLLARD

The Fiore Amaro was inspired by a Campari, strawberry, and black pepper sorbet. This is a great option if you're the type of person who likes to drink their dessert.

1 strawberry, hulled

1½ ounces (45 ml) Campari

¾ ounce (22.5 ml) fresh lemon juice

¾ ounce (22.5 ml) Black Pepper Syrup (page 242)

¾ ounce (22.5 ml) Luxardo maraschino liqueur

Add the strawberry to the tin of a cocktail shaker and muddle. Add the remaining ingredients, fill the shaker glass with ice, then shake until chilled. Double-strain into a chilled cocktail glass and serve.

SEA DOG

KIRK ESTOPINAL

If you've made Kirk's excellent but questionably named Esgana Cão (page 65) and are looking for more ways to use the bottle of Madeira you bought, here's your drink. It's a simple, refreshing cobbler with an electric acidity that reminds me of lemon curd and does what a cobbler should do: elevate the base spirit. "When I worked at the Violet Hour, Toby Maloney really instilled in me that cobblers and Old-Fashioneds should uplift certain aspects of the bottle. So I don't go crazy; I keep it linear and clean," Kirk explains.

1½ ounces (45 ml) Rare Wine Co. Charleston Sercial Madeira

½ ounce (15 ml) Simple Syrup (page 243)

2 lemon peels

1 orange peel

17 drops Bittermens Xocolatl mole bitters, including 7 for garnish

Combine all the ingredients except the garnish in a shaker with 5 cracked ice cubes and shake until chilled. Dump the contents of the shaker (including the ice—no need to strain) into a double-old fashioned glass, garnish with the 7 drops of mole bitters, and serve.

FIORE AMARO

Any book about New Orleans that doesn't talk about food is immediately suspect. I don't care if it's a book about jazz or politics or native plant species. There will 100 percent be a connection to New Orleans food culture.

So I knew I had to include some food recipes in this book, since a person can't live on cocktails alone. I tapped some of the most talented chefs working on the New Orleans scene, all of whom happen to be friends of mine, and asked them to share their favorite things to eat alongside a cocktail. These dishes run the gamut: an elevated version of deviled eggs; deep-fried rice fritters (you'll notice a lot of deep-fried dishes . . . it is New Orleans, after all); a steak tartare with smoked oysters. Next time you host a New Orleans–themed cocktail party, make sure to serve a snack or two from this chapter along with your Sazeracs and gin fizzes.

DEVILED EGGS "CACIO E PEPE"

ALFREDO NOGUEIRA

MAKES 12

....

1 head garlic

Extra-virgin olive oil

6 large eggs

¼ cup (60 ml) mayonnaise

½ teaspoon Dijon mustard

2 dashes Tabasco sauce, or to taste

Kosher salt

Freshly grated Pecorino Romano
   cheese

Freshly ground black pepper

One of the many reasons we're lucky to have Chef Alfredo Nogueira at the helm of the kitchens at CureCo. is that he elevates even the simplest bar snacks into something special. Take, for example, deviled eggs, a staple at every Southern potluck. Turns out, if you pulse the egg yolk mixture into a creamy filling accented with Dijon and rich roasted garlic, then shower the finished eggs with Italian Pecorino Romano and black pepper, then it's a whole new ballgame.

Preheat the oven to 400°F (205°C). Remove the loose, papery outer layer of the garlic but leave the majority unpeeled. Trim away the top ¼ inch (6 mm) of the bulb, then drizzle it all over with the olive oil. Wrap tightly in foil and roast for 40 minutes to 1 hour, or until a center clove is completely soft when pierced with a knife.

Remove the garlic from the oven and set aside 2 cloves of garlic for the deviled eggs. (The rest can be spread on bread or used in place of raw garlic in dressings and condiments.)

Bring a large pot of water to a boil and prepare an ice-water bath. Use a slotted spoon or spider skimmer to place the eggs in the water and adjust the heat to maintain a gentle simmer. Cook the eggs for 11 minutes, then immediately drain and transfer them to the ice-water bath. Once cool, peel the eggs and trim a small slice off the short sides of each egg so that it's flat on both ends (this will make it easier to plate them). Slice each egg in half crosswise.

Use a spoon to scoop out the yolks and place them in the bowl of a food processor. Add the mayonnaise, mustard, the 2 cloves of roasted garlic, and Tabasco and season with salt. Process until creamy and well blended. Adjust the salt if needed.

At this stage you can transfer the yolk mixture to a pastry bag with a star tip or just transfer it to a standard zip-top bag and snip away one of the corners. Pipe the yolk mixture into the reserved egg whites. Arrange the filled egg halves on a serving plate, sprinkle with the Pecorino Romano and black pepper, and serve.

CRAWFISH CROQUETAS

ALFREDO NOGUEIRA

SERVES 6 TO 8

....

1 cup (2 sticks / 225 g) unsalted
   butter

1 medium onion, diced

1 cup (125 g) all-purpose flour

2 cups (480 ml) milk

8 ounces (225 g) cooked crawfish
   tail meat, chopped

½ bunch flat-leaf parsley, chopped

Juice from ½ lemon

Kosher salt

Freshly cracked black pepper

3 medium eggs, lightly beaten

2 cups (200 g) Italian-style bread
   crumbs

Canola oil, for frying

This is a classic Cane & Table dish: Southern with a bit of Cuban influence. What's not to like about crawfish, béchamel, and fried goodness? If you poke around, you can probably find frozen crawfish tails in most places in the U.S., but feel free to sub cooked Gulf shrimp for the crawfish if you'd like. At the restaurant, we serve this with aioli for dipping.

In a large skillet over medium-low heat, melt the butter. Add the onion and sauté until translucent, about 7 minutes. Add the flour and cook, stirring constantly to ensure nothing sticks, until you have a sandy-colored roux, about 8 minutes. Add the milk in a steady stream, whisking constantly to ensure it is well integrated. Reduce the heat to low and cook, stirring occasionally, until the liquid has become thick and tight. Stir in the crawfish meat, then remove from the heat and stir in the parsley and lemon juice. Season with salt and pepper to taste.

Coat a baking sheet with a thin film of canola oil and spread the crawfish béchamel mixture over it. Cover it with plastic wrap to prevent a skin from forming, then refrigerate until chilled and firm, 1 to 2 hours.

Set up your dredging station: Place the eggs in one bowl and the bread crumbs in another. Season the bread crumbs with salt and pepper. Roll the chilled crawfish béchamel into 1-inch (2.25-cm) balls, then, working one at a time, roll each ball into the bread crumbs, dip it into the egg wash (allowing any excess to drip off), then roll it once again in the bread crumbs.

In a large heavy-bottomed pan or Dutch oven, pour the oil to a depth of 1½ inches (4 cm). Heat the oil over medium-high heat until it registers 365°F (185°C) on a deep-fry or candy thermometer. Working in batches so as not to crowd the pan, fry the croquetas, turning them once, until they are deep golden brown, about 3 minutes. Transfer to a paper towel–lined plate to drain, then repeat with the remaining croquetas. Serve immediately.

Bar Snacks

PIMENTO CHEESE WITH B&B PICKLES AND PEPPER JELLY

ALFREDO NOGUEIRA

SERVES 8 TO 10; MAKES ABOUT 1½ CUPS (360 ML) CHEESE

8 ounces (225 g) Hooks 2-Year cheddar (or another high-quality aged cheddar), grated

¼ cup (60 ml) mayonnaise

1½ ounces (40 g) cream cheese, at room temperature

¼ cup (60 g) diced roasted piquillo peppers

1½ teaspoons hot sauce

½ teaspoon Worcestershire sauce

¼ teaspoon freshly ground black pepper

¼ teaspoon garlic powder

¼ teaspoon onion powder

¼ teaspoon paprika

⅛ teaspoon cayenne

Kosher salt

Saltines or thinly sliced, toasted baguette, for serving

Bread and butter pickles, for serving

Pepper jelly, for serving

Pimento cheese is polarizing. My dad has a soft spot for any mayo-drenched salad—egg salad, chicken salad, tuna salad, pimento cheese—and he also couldn't really cook, so I associate pimento cheese with the grim meals he'd make us when my mom was away. (Vienna sausages figured prominently.) If you have similar reservations about pimento cheese, get rid of them now. Fredo's version is incredible, made with a high-quality cheddar and a hint of smoky paprika.

Combine the cheese, mayonnaise, cream cheese, diced piquillos, hot sauce, Worcestershire, black pepper, garlic powder, onion powder, paprika, and cayenne in the bowl of a stand mixer fitted with the paddle attachment. Mix on low speed until well incorporated, then season with salt to taste.

Using an ice cream scoop or two spoons, scoop out a portion of cheese onto a serving plate along with the saltines or baguette, pickles, and pepper jelly. Any leftover pimento cheese can be stored airtight in the refrigerator for up to 1 week.

STEAK TARTARE WITH SMOKED OYSTER MAYONNAISE

RYAN PREWITT

SERVES 6

6 oysters in the shell (or sub high-quality tinned smoked oysters)

3/4 cup (180 ml) mayonnaise

Ciabatta or another rustic bread, for serving

1 pound (455 g) top-quality sirloin, trimmed of any sinew

2 tablespoons Tartare Base (recipe on following page)

4 egg yolks

2 teaspoons kosher salt

½ teaspoon freshly ground black pepper

¼ cup (15 g) fresh parsley, thinly sliced

½ cup (50 g) celery hearts, thinly sliced, plus more for garnish

1 tablespoon fresh lemon juice

Ryan is the chef at Pêche Seafood Grill, which he opened with chefs Donald Link and Stephen Stryjewski in 2013. Ryan also happens to be one of the coolest guys on the planet. I am honored to be on a text thread with him and a few other food industry people where we share images of the best hotel club sandwiches we encounter in our travels. Of course, this recipe isn't for a club sandwich. Nor is it for a seafood dish, which is Pêche's specialty.

To me, Ryan's standout dish is his steak tartare, and I always order it when I visit the restaurant. I love all the celery notes, but the smoked oyster mayonnaise is what makes it truly special. If you don't like the food at Pêche, all I can tell you is your tongue is broken.

To make the oyster mayonnaise, heat a smoker to 200°F (95°C). Shuck the oysters, removing and discarding the top shells but taking care to leave the oysters and their juices in the bottom shells. Place the oysters in their bottom shells on the smoker, close the lid tightly, and cook until the oysters are firm to the touch and have taken on the color of the smoke. (Alternatively, you can use tinned smoked oysters.) Cool the oysters completely, then add the oyster meat and juices and the mayonnaise to a food processor and puree. Set the mayonnaise aside while you prepare the toast and tartare.

Cut the ciabatta into 2-inch (5-cm) slices, then toast. Set aside until ready to serve.

To make the tartare, slice the sirloin very thinly, then dice it as finely as you can. In a large bowl, combine the sirloin, tartare base, egg yolks, salt, pepper, parsley, celery hearts, and lemon juice and stir until integrated. Taste and adjust seasoning as needed. To serve, smear a generous spoonful of the oyster mayonnaise on each piece of bread, top with a dollop of tartare, and sprinkle additional celery hearts over the top.

Tartare Base

MAKES ½ CUP (120 ML)

....

3 cloves garlic, minced

3 anchovy fillets, minced

2 tablespoons capers, rinsed and minced

3 tablespoons Dijon mustard

½ teaspoon Tabasco

¼ teaspoon Worcestershire sauce

Combine all the ingredients in a mini chopper and purée into a paste. Alternatively, chop the garlic, anchovies, and capers into a fine paste, add to a bowl with the mustard, Tabasco, and Worcestershire, and stir to combine.

CURE

PICKLED SHRIMP WITH CELERY AND BUTTERMILK

NINA COMPTON

SERVES 6 TO 8

For the court bouillon:

2 stalks celery, cut into 2-inch
(5-cm) pieces

½ yellow onion, cut into 2-inch
(5-cm) pieces

½ fennel bulb, cut into 2-inch
(5-cm) pieces

½ cup (120 ml) white wine

2 tablespoons kosher salt

Juice of 1 lemon

Juice of 1 lime

Juice of 1 orange

1 pound (455 g) whole head-on,
shell-on Gulf shrimp, U-10
(see Note on page 234)

3 cups (720 ml) rice vinegar

1 cup (240 ml) Buttermilk
Dressing (recipe on page 234)

1¼ cups rye croutons
(approximately ½-inch / 12 mm
square)

2 small avocados, diced into 1-inch
(2.5 cm) pieces

2 stalks celery, peeled and sliced
½ inch (12 mm) thick

1 teaspoon celery seeds

What can I say about Nina that hasn't already been said? She's a fucking icon, and I have so much respect for her. In New Orleans it can be hard for people from outside the city to break in. Nina was born and raised on the Caribbean island of St. Lucia. But Nina didn't just "break in" when she opened her debut New Orleans restaurant, Compère Lapin—she was a smash. She understood New Orleans so well, but also didn't pander to us or try to cater to our perceived "tastes." She brought her unique style and flavors, and guess what? We loved it. I'd argue that her restaurant opening was one of the most impressive of my lifetime.

Make the court bouillon: In a large saucepan, combine the celery, onion, fennel, wine, and salt with 1 quart (1 liter) cold water and bring to a boil over high heat. Reduce heat to a simmer and cook for 20 minutes. Add the lemon, lime, and orange juice and simmer for an additional 10 minutes. Strain into a wide saucepan and keep warm over medium-low heat.

Skewer the shrimp onto wooden dowels so they stay straight while cooking. Adjust the heat of the court bouillon so it is just below a simmer. Poach the shrimp in the warm court bouillon for 3 to 5 minutes, or until the flesh is opaque. Transfer to an ice water bath until fully chilled, 5 to 10 minutes. Once chilled, peel the shrimp and discard the heads and shells (or save them for stock). Marinate the shrimp in the rice vinegar for 30 minutes, then strain and reserve ½ cup of the rice vinegar.

Devein the shrimp and cut them in half lengthwise, then slice into thirds on the bias.

Place the buttermilk dressing on the bottom of a serving platter or divide evenly between serving bowls. Top with the croutons.

Continued

Bar Snacks

½ cup (120 ml) olive oil

3 ounces (85 g) trout roe

½ jalapeño (or more to taste), thinly sliced and soaked in ice water for 10 minutes

1 radish, thinly sliced and soaked in ice water for 10 minutes

Celery leaves (saved from the celery hearts), for garnish

Flaky sea salt (such as Maldon), for garnish

Chili oil, optional

In a large mixing bowl, combine the shrimp, avocado, celery, and celery seeds and season to taste with salt. Add the reserved ½ cup (120 ml) vinegar, olive oil, and trout roe, then taste and adjust seasoning. Place the dressed shrimp over the buttermilk and croutons, then top with the jalapeño and radish. Garnish with the celery leaves and sea salt, drizzle the chili oil around the exposed rim of the buttermilk dressing, and serve.

Note: If you cannot find head-on shrimp, substitute ¾ pound of shell-on shrimp without their heads.

Buttermilk Dressing

MAKES ABOUT 2 CUPS (480 ML)

....

¼ cup (60 ml) mayonnaise

1 cup (240 ml) buttermilk

1 teaspoon Dijon mustard

1 clove garlic

½ cup (50 g) Parmigiano-Reggiano, grated

1 tablespoon red wine vinegar

1½ teaspoons Worcestershire

½ teaspoon freshly ground white pepper

1 teaspoon kosher salt

½ anchovy fillet

1 teaspoon lemon juice

Place all the dressing ingredients in a blender and puree until smooth. Store airtight in the refrigerator for up to 3 days.

LI'L SMOKIES MINI CORN DOGS

MASON HEREFORD

SERVES 8

Vegetable oil, for deep frying

1 (14-ounce / 400-g) package L'il Smokies miniature hot dogs

4 dozen toothpicks

2 cups (250 g) all-purpose flour

1 cup (180 g) fine yellow cornmeal

¼ cup (50 g) white sugar

1½ teaspoons baking powder

1 teaspoon baking soda

1 teaspoon kosher salt

1¼ cups (300 ml) well-shaken buttermilk

1 medium egg, lightly beaten

1 cup (240 ml) yellow mustard, for serving

Mason is the chef and owner of Turkey and the Wolf, a sandwich shop in the Irish Channel, and Molly's Rise and Shine, a breakfast spot just down the street. But those descriptions don't do justice to these wild and wonderful restaurants. Mason is definitely some sort of mad genius. He takes a lot of kitschy or nostalgic ingredients and elevates them; for example, cocktail wienies. After you batter and fry them in this corn dog preparation, you'll be asking yourself why you ever stopped buying Li'l Smokies.

Preheat the oven to 250°F (120°C) and line a sheet pan with a wire rack or paper towels. Heat about 4 inches (10 cm) of the oil in a heavy-bottomed pot and set it over medium-high heat until it registers 350°F (175°C) on a deep-fry thermometer.

While the oil is heating up, get set up: Skewer each dog on a toothpick, stopping before the point pokes through the dog. Place 1 cup (125 g) of the flour on a large plate, then roll the hot dogs around to coat them in the flour, shaking off any excess. In a medium bowl, combine the cornmeal, sugar, baking powder, baking soda, salt, and the remaining cup (125 g) of flour, stir well, then add the buttermilk and egg and whisk until smooth. Pour it into a tall glass for easy battering.

When the oil reaches 350°F (175°C), start battering and frying the dogs. You'll do this in batches of about 10 at a time (make sure you don't crowd the pan). Dip 1 dog in the batter to evenly coat it, giving the toothpick a little twirl as you lift it out to make sure the dog is covered. Working quickly but also carefully so you don't burn yourself, gently lower the battered dog into the frying oil, then repeat with more hot dogs. Fry the first batch until the crusts have a nice grocery bag–brown color, 3 to 5 minutes. Using a spider skimmer or slotted spoon, transfer the dogs to the sheet pan and pop it in the oven to keep them warm, then fry the rest of the dogs in batches, adding them to the sheet pan as they're done.

Serve warm with the mustard.

SHRIMP CALAS

FRANK BRIGTSEN

MAKES 24

2 tablespoons unsalted butter

1 pound (455 g) peeled shrimp

2 teaspoons Chef Paul Prudhomme's Seafood Magic seasoning

½ cup (30 g) thinly sliced green onions

1½ teaspoons minced garlic

4 medium eggs

½ cup (120 ml) milk

1 cup (125 g) all-purpose flour

1 tablespoon baking powder

1 tablespoon white sugar

1 teaspoon kosher salt

4 cups (800 g) cooked rice

Canola oil or another neutral oil, for deep-frying

I'm sure this will make Frank feel old, but I've been going to Brigtsen's since I was a child. It is truly one of the most special places in the world. When you visit this neighborhood restaurant in the Riverbend, Frank, his wife, Marna, and their sisters Sandy and Rhonda make you feel like you're part of their family. Frank has been a keeper of the flame for traditional New Orleans cooking for decades, and if you visit New Orleans, you cannot skip Brigtsen's.

Here, Frank shares his recipe for calas, Creole rice cakes with origins in Africa. "They are made with leftover cooked rice and were originally served as a sweet treat, dusted with powdered sugar," Frank explains. "This is a savory version made with Louisiana shrimp, but you can flavor the calas mix with many things, including andouille sausage or crawfish."

Melt the butter in a saucepan over medium-high heat. Add the shrimp and cook, stirring constantly, just until the shrimp turn pink on the outside, 1 to 2 minutes. Add the seafood seasoning, green onions, and garlic and cook until the shrimp are fully cooked and opaque, 1 to 2 minutes more. Transfer the shrimp mixture to the refrigerator to chill completely.

Transfer half the shrimp to a food processor and puree. Coarsely chop the remaining shrimp and set aside.

Crack the eggs into a large bowl and whisk until frothy. Add the milk and whisk until fully blended. Add the flour, baking powder, sugar, and salt and whisk until smooth. Add the cooked rice, pureed shrimp, and chopped shrimp and fold with a spatula until fully combined. Cover and refrigerate until chilled.

To cook the calas, fill a large heavy-bottomed pot or Dutch oven halfway with the canola oil. Heat the oil over medium-high heat until it registers 350°F (190°C) on a deep-fry thermometer. Using a 2-ounce (60-ml) scoop or two tablespoons, form the calas into 3- to 4-tablespoon mounds and fry until cooked through, about 5 minutes. Set on paper towels to drain. Serve immediately.

BLUE CRAB BEIGNETS

JUSTIN DEVILLIER

MAKES 6 TO 8

½ small shallot, finely chopped

6 ounces (170 g) fresh blue
  crabmeat, picked over for shells

⅓ cup (75 ml) mascarpone

1 tablespoon finely chopped chives

½ teaspoon kosher salt, plus more
  to taste

Vegetable oil, for frying

1 cup (125 g) all-purpose flour

⅓ cup (45 g) cornstarch

1 tablespoon baking powder

1 cup (240 ml) amber lager

This is the one dish I have to order every single time I go to La Petite Grocery. The beignets are so light and airy, and once you have one, there is no turning back. According to Justin, they're the most popular dish that's ever been on his menu. As he says in his book, *The New Orleans Kitchen*, "What's not to love? It's essentially a cheesy crab doughnut."

In a medium bowl, combine the shallot, crabmeat, mascarpone, and chives and season with salt. Gently fold to combine, then cover and place in the refrigerator until chilled.

When ready to fry, pour the oil into a large, heavy-bottomed pot or Dutch oven to a depth of at least 3 inches (7.5 cm). Heat the oil over medium-high heat until it reaches 375°F (190°C).

Meanwhile, in a large bowl, make the batter by whisking together the flour, cornstarch, baking powder, and the ½ teaspoon salt. Gradually whisk in the lager, just to blend (the batter will be thick).

Measure 1 heaping tablespoon of the crab mixture, roll it into a ball, and drop into the batter. Using a fork, toss to coat, then lift from the batter, letting the excess drip back into bowl.

Working in batches of about four at a time and returning the oil to 375°F (190°C) each time, fry the beignets, turning occasionally, until crisp and deep golden brown, about 4 minutes. Transfer to a paper towel–lined plate to drain, season with salt, and serve hot.

Bar Snacks

MUSSELS IN ABSINTHE

KRISTEN ESSIG

SERVES 6

For the poached mussels:

5 pounds (2.3 kg) mussels, scrubbed and debearded

2 tablespoons extra-virgin olive oil

3 sprigs thyme

¼ cup (60 ml) dry white wine

For the absinthe marinade:

¼ cup (60 ml) reserved mussel broth

¼ cup (60 ml) Herbsaint

1 large shallot, thinly shaved

2 large sprigs thyme, leaves stripped from the stems and lightly chopped

2 cloves garlic, thinly shaved

¾ cup extra-virgin olive oil

¼ teaspoon freshly ground black pepper

Juice and zest of 1 lemon

To serve:

Crème fraiche

Fried saltines (see Note)

Kristen is an amazing chef and dear friend who we were lucky to lure to Washington, D.C., to be the opening chef at our restaurant Dauphine's. Her mind moves so fast, and you can sense the level of detail she puts into every dish—yet she maintains a light touch, and the food always tastes pure. This mussels dish is a perfect example. Every ingredient has its place and elevates what seems like a simple preparation to something with deep New Orleans soul.

Discard any mussels with cracked shells or that are opened. In a large pot, heat the oil over medium-high. Add the mussels and thyme sprigs to the pot and pour the wine over the top. Cover the pot and cook 3 to 5 minutes, shaking the pot (with the lid on) once or twice during cooking. After 3 minutes, check the mussels. Most should be open by now—if not, re-cover and cook for an additional 1 to 2 minutes. Discard any mussels that still haven't opened by this time and shell the remainder. Place the mussel meat in a bowl and store in the refrigerator. Save ¼ cup (60 ml) of the mussel cooking broth. Discard the shells.

In a large bowl, combine all the marinade ingredients, stirring to mix. Add the mussels, cover, and refrigerate for at least 4 hours and up to overnight.

To serve, remove the mussels from the refrigerator to take a bit of the chill off. Serve with crème fraiche and fried saltines.

Note: To fry saltines, heat some neutral oil in a high-sided sauté pan to 350°F (175°C). Fry the saltines (working in batches as necessary so as not to crowd the pan) until golden, 2 to 3 minutes. Drain on paper towels before serving.

SYRUPS AND OTHER HOUSE-MADE INGREDIENTS

Agave Syrup

2 parts raw agave nectar

1 part boiling water

Combine in a nonreactive container and stir until dissolved. Store airtight in the refrigerator for up to 4 weeks.

Black Pepper Syrup

MAKES ABOUT
1 CUP (240 ML)

1 cup (200 g) white sugar

1 cup (240 ml) water

¼ cup (24 g) freshly ground black pepper

Combine all the ingredients in a small saucepan and bring to a boil. Reduce heat to a simmer and cook for 5 minutes. Double-strain, multiple times if needed, until there are no particles left and the syrup is clear. Transfer to a nonreactive container. Store airtight in the refrigerator for up to 4 weeks.

Cinnamon Syrup

MAKES ABOUT
1 CUP (240 ML)

1 cup (240 ml) water

3 cinnamon sticks

1 cup (200 g) white sugar

Combine the water and cinnamon in a small saucepan and bring to a boil. Cover, reduce the heat to a simmer, and cook for 20 minutes. Add the sugar and stir until dissolved. Remove from heat, let sit for at least 1 hour and up to 4 hours, then strain into a nonreactive container. Store airtight in the refrigerator for up to 4 weeks.

Demerara Syrup

2 parts Demerara sugar

1 part water

Combine the sugar and water in a small saucepan and bring to a boil. At the first crack of a boil, remove from the heat and continue stirring until dissolved. Let cool then transfer to a nonreactive container. Store airtight in the refrigerator for up to 4 weeks.

Ginger Syrup

1 part fresh ginger juice

1 part white sugar

Combine the ginger juice and sugar in a blender. Blend until smooth and combined, then fine-strain into a nonreactive container. Store airtight in the refrigerator for up to 2 weeks.

Grenadine

MAKES ABOUT
1 QUART (1 LITER)

2½ cups (600 ml) pomegranate juice

1½ cups (360 ml) Simple Syrup (page 243)

½ cup (120 ml) brandy

14 drops orange flower water

Combine the pomegranate juice and 1 cup (120 ml) of the simple syrup in a medium saucepan and bring to a boil. Cook until reduced by ½ cup (120 ml), then remove from the heat and stir in the brandy, orange flower water, and remaining ½ cup (120 ml) simple syrup. Let cool then transfer to a nonreactive container and store airtight in the refrigerator for up to 2 weeks.

Honey Syrup

2 parts honey

1 part boiling water

Combine in a nonreactive container and stir until dissolved. Store airtight in the refrigerator for up to 4 weeks.

Lemon-Orange Oleo Syrup

MAKES ABOUT
1 CUP (240 ML)

Peels of 2 lemons

Peel of 1 orange

1 cup (200 g) white sugar

1 cup (240 ml) hot water

Combine the peels and sugar in a nonreactive container and let rest in a warm, dark place for at least 8 hours and up to 48 hours. Add the hot water and stir until the sugar dissolves. Once cool, fine-strain into a nonreactive container. Store airtight in the refrigerator for up to 4 weeks.

Orgeat

2 cups (280 g) raw almonds

1 part unsweetened almond milk

1 part white sugar

1 part Demerara sugar

Rosewater, to taste

Orange flower water, to taste

Preheat the oven to 350°F (165°C). Spread the almonds in an even layer on a baking sheet and toast, shaking the pan once during cooking, 8 to 12 minutes, or until fragrant.

Meanwhile, combine the almond milk and sugars in a medium saucepan and bring to a low simmer over medium heat. Stir until the sugars have dissolved, then remove from the heat. Add the toasted almonds and allow to cool to room temperature, then add rosewater and orange flower water to taste. Strain into a nonreactive container and store airtight in the fridge for up to 2 weeks.

Saline Solution

1 part Maldon sea salt

2 parts water

Combine the salt and water in a saucepan and bring to a simmer over medium-high heat. Once the salt is dissolved, remove from the heat and allow to cool. Transfer to a nonreactive container and store airtight in the fridge for up to 4 weeks.

Simple Syrup

1 part white sugar

1 part cold water

Combine in a blender and puree until the sugar is dissolved, or combine in a nonreactive lidded jar and shake until the sugar is dissolved. Store airtight in the refrigerator for up to 4 weeks.

COCKTAIL CONTRIBUTORS

ALEX ANDERSON moved from Atlanta to New Orleans, where she was an integral part of the Cure team that won a James Beard Award for best bar program in America. She now resides in Portland, Oregon, with a curiously social cat named Love. Alex is currently behind the bar at Takibi.

COLIN BUGBEE has been at Cure for five years and counting. He was promoted to head bartender in 2020 and describes himself as "more of a dog lover than a people person."

TURK DIETRICH was on the opening team at Cure and was the general manager for seven years leading up to COVID-19. He is now a partner in Vals with some of the other CureCo. folks.

RHIANNON ENLIL moved to New Orleans in 2000, bartended for many years, and developed a passion for beverage history and education. She was part of the opening team at Cure and considers those years some of the most valuable of her career. She still misses the soundtrack.

KIRK ESTOPINAL is a New Orleans–born ex-bartender and current partner in Cure and Cane & Table. He is the co-creator of the *Rogue* and *Beta Cocktails* books, the father of two, and husband of Melanie Kunz.

RYAN GANNON spent seven years at Cure and now lives and works in New York City.

RICKY GOMEZ was part of the opening team at Cure. He currently resides in Portland, Oregon, where he owns and operates Palomar, a Cuban-inspired cocktail bar and restaurant.

NICHOLAS JARRETT spent the better part of a decade behind the stick at Cure. Previously, he was a bartender at the Franklin in Philadelphia and at Dram, Clover Club, and Flatiron Lounge in New York City. He is currently head bartender of Peychaud's in the French Quarter.

LIZ KELLEY began her hospitality career in her hometown of Louisville, Kentucky. She is a bartender at Cure and has been a part of the team since 2018.

BRADEN LAGRONE is from Shreveport, Louisiana, and worked around the state before finding a place in New Orleans and eventually at Cure, where he worked for almost four years. He was also part of the opening staff at Cane & Table.

MATT LOFINK moved from Philly to New Orleans in 2014 and started at CureCo. shortly after his arrival. He bartended at Cure for many years and says the greatest honor of his life was serving as co-bar manager. During his time there, he fell in love with the world of spirits and now works as the central spirits specialist for Frederick Wildman Imports and as an ambassador for Chartreuse Liqueur. His boss, Neal Bodenheimer, gave him the nickname "Machine" due to his hard-nosed work ethic and inability to smile.

GENEVIEVE MASHBURN considers her years with Cure an especially treasured chapter of her hospitality career for the professional prowess, lessons about life and spirits, and enduring friendships forged therein. These days, you can find her wrangling horses, flowers, and booze across the coastal South and beyond.

MAKSYM PAZUNIAK is co-owner of Jupiter Disco, a cocktail bar in Brooklyn, New York, and co-author of the *Rogue* and *Beta Cocktails* book series. A former New Orleans resident, Maks was on Cure's opening team and later worked at the Counting Room and Maison Premiere in New York before opening Jupiter Disco in late 2016.

CHRISTINA RANDO takes a culinary approach to making cocktails, drawing inspiration from dishes that she loves and is inspired by. For the last thirteen years, this has been her

methodology, and it will likely continue on for the duration of her career.

MORGAN SULLIVAN is a bartender, spirits educator, and beverage consultant. Professionally, she seeks opportunities to mentor, educate, and create innovative ways to explore the palate.

DANNY VALDÉZ is an acclaimed photographer, artist, spirits educator, and raconteur whose philanthropic endeavors have become his main focus. Proceeds of his photography books and art projects have been dedicated to various charitable organizations. "Live to serve, serve to live."

MATT YOUNG, born in New Orleans and raised in Madison, Wisconsin, is a bartender and graphic designer. He credits his mom, Nancy (and her annual basil harvest and pesto-making), with introducing him to the beauty of the culinary arts.

MICHAEL YUSKO was born in Hudson, New York. His father was the mayor during most of his youth. He got beat up a lot for it. He moved to New Orleans thirteen years ago because of a girl. They are currently married with two kids. He will never live in Paris or Berlin. Michael's first job in New Orleans was at Cure. Over the last decade, he's done damn good work in the cocktail field. He's currently unemployed and hopes to never bartend again.

RESOURCES

Barware, Glassware, and Accessories

BARFLY BY MERCER
barflybymercer.com

BOTTESI
bottesi.es

COCKTAIL KINGDOM
cocktailkingdom.com

KUHN RIKON
kuhnrikonshop.com

TWELVE24
1224cocktails.com

UMAMI MART
umamimart.com

VISKI
viski.com

Spirits

The best bet is always an independent wine and spirits shop in your area—support local small businesses! For online purchases, check out the following retailers:

ASTOR WINES & SPIRITS
astorwines.com

BINNY'S BEVERAGE DEPOT
binnys.com

K&L WINE MERCHANTS
klwines.com

RESERVEBAR
reservebar.com

UPTOWN SPIRITS
uptownspirits.com

THE WHISKY EXCHANGE
thewhiskyexchange.com

ACKNOWLEDGMENTS

I never thought that I would or could be a part of creating a book from start to finish, and I know for certain that this book would never have seen the light of day without two very important women, Kea Sherman and Emily Timberlake.

As Cure crosses into its thirteenth year of existence, I have become acutely aware that my closest thought partner has been my extraordinary life partner, Kea Sherman. Kea pushed me to explore the book even when I really didn't want to and didn't think it was a possibility. I'm a pretty stubborn person, so I'm not exaggerating when I say that this book never would have happened without her persistence and encouragement. In fact, while sharing a car home from an event with Mia and Justin Devillier, Kea asked Justin how he got his book made and he said, "Just call David Black; that's all you need to do." Amazingly, Justin was right, David Black liked the idea, and the rest is history. Thank you, Mia and Justin!

What can I say about Emily Timberlake? I could just say that Emily is the best, but that wouldn't encapsulate how remarkable a human she is and how she took an amorphous idea and sculpted it into something that we are both genuinely proud of. Basically, Emily transformed me from a literary perspective in the same way that Michael Caine transformed Steve Martin in *Dirty Rotten Scoundrels*. No small task, I can assure you. Not only would this book not have been made without Emily, but I feel certain that if some other poor soul had taken the charge, it wouldn't have been nearly as good. As a side note, our weekly Zooms during the pandemic definitely helped me keep my sanity! I feel truly grateful that the Cure book brought Emily into my life.

A huge thank you to Denny Culbert, who effortlessly made everything he put in his viewfinder look even better than reality. Denny, you are an amazing talent and we have been so honored to get to work with you. I'm sorry you had to sacrifice your car to the gods in the name of this book.

A big thanks to the Cure team past and present for their hard work, commitment, and talent (as evidenced by the amazing number of stellar recipes in this book). You know who you are. This has been a collective effort just like Cure has been from the first day. I said it when we won the James Beard Award and I'll say it again: We can achieve more together than apart, and this once again is proof. Thank you for your stellar work and contributions over the years.

Thank you to my business partners in Cure, Matthew Kohnke and Kirk Estopinal. Thank you to Katherine England and Turk Dietrich for being a part of Cure from the very beginning. Thank you to Mom, Dad, Carey, and Peter, and all of our friends and family for the support through good times and bad. To my daughter Hayden, this book is for you. I wanted to put something in the historical record for you, and I hope when you're older that you take pride in this book (while also using it in moderation).

Thank you to Alfredo Nogueira and Morgan Sullivan for literally producing every dish and cocktail in this book and making them all look amazing. Thank you to all of our friends who participated in the book: Katy Casbarian, L. Kasimu Harris, Annene Kaye-Berry, Jeff Berry, Pableaux Johnson, Ian Neville, Nina Compton, Frank Brigtsen, Kelly Fields, Justin Devillier, Kristen Essig, Ryan Prewitt, Mason Hereford, and Alfredo Nogueira (again).

A big thank you to Gia Vecchio for consistent guidance, friendship, and support through this process. Thank you to David Black and his entire team. What can I say that others haven't? David took a very hard and complex process and made it easy enough that even a rube like me could feel good about it.

Thank you to Laura Dozier and the Abrams team for seeing potential in this little book of ours and believing in it enough to let us make it. We are so grateful for your partnership and guidance throughout this process and for the many, many contributions your team has made to turn it from good to great.

I know I'm forgetting people, but there are so many people who I love and/or who have positively influenced the book. I'm sorry if I've missed you, but there is a word limit on this sucker.

—NEAL BODENHEIMER

First and most importantly, thank you to Neal Bodenheimer for being the best part of a very . . . ahem, *weird* couple of years. Can you believe I actually looked forward to our calls? How dare you make me excited to work! But I always knew I would learn so much from you and get in enough laughs to sustain me for the rest of the week. So thank you for inviting me into the world of Cure, and trusting me with this wonderful story.

Thanks also to our brilliant photographer, Denny Culbert, a man I knew I wanted to work with from the first moment I first heard the words "New Orleans cocktail book." Thank you for blessing this project with your many talents. There is no person I'd rather drive around with in a tiny rental car full of photo gear and sourdough starter. Thanks also to Emily Ferretti for her help, feedback, and boundless positive energy. For what it's worth, I did not think you were cursed.

We couldn't have made this book without Morgan Sullivan, who mixed and styled every drink you see in these pages, and whose technical prowess and impeccable aesthetic were invaluable. You are this book's secret weapon! Thank you!

Thank you to all the chefs who generously contributed recipes to this book, and especially to Fredo Nogueira, who cooked and styled all the beautiful food in Chapter 9. More importantly, he fed us delicious tacos while we were on set and wrote what is hands down the best croqueta and pimento cheese recipes I have ever tasted.

Thank you to David Black and Rica Allanic, the best damn literary agents in the biz: We are so lucky to be a part of your team.

Thank you to everyone at Abrams books: Our editor, Laura Dozier, who fielded my unhinged phone calls and emails about metric conversions with patience and grace; Heesang Lee, who developed the gorgeous design; Deb Wood; Mike Richards; Denise LaCongo; Natasha Martin; Kevin Callahan; Mamie VanLangen; Lauren Purcell; Sarah Scheffel; Chris Cerasi; and Laura Cooke.

Thank you to Ted, MaryGael, and Teddy Timberlake for being my favorite people on the planet.

And of course, thank you to Ethan Forrest for being a top-five Louisianan and number-one husband. Peace and love.

—EMILY TIMBERLAKE

INDEX

Note: Page numbers in *italics* include photos and/or photo captions. Page numbers in **bold** indicate Contributor's biographical sketches.

CURE

Editor: Laura Dozier
Managing Editor: Mike Richards
Designer: Heesang Lee
Production Manager: Denise LaCongo

Library of Congress Control Number: 2022933506

ISBN: 978-1-4197-5852-2
eISBN: 978-1-64700-856-7

Printed and bound in China

10 9 8 7 6 5 4 3 2

Abrams books are available at special discounts when
purchased in quantity for premiums and promotions as well
as fundraising or educational use. Special editions can also
be created to specification. For details, contact
specialsales@abramsbooks.com or the address below.

Abrams® is a registered trademark of Harry N. Abrams, Inc.

ABRAMS The Art of Books
195 Broadway, New York, NY 10007
abramsbooks.com

ABOUT THE AUTHORS

NEAL BODENHEIMER was born and raised in New Orleans. In 2009, he opened his first cocktail bar, Cure, on a flood-damaged stretch of Freret Street. Since then, Cure has become an international cocktail destination, and won a James Beard Award for Best Bar Program. Bodenheimer also owns local bars and restaurants Cane & Table, Vals, Peychaud's, and Dauphine's in Washington, D.C. He is co-chair of the Tales of the Cocktail Foundation, a nonprofit organization that educates, advances, and supports the global hospitality industry.

EMILY TIMBERLAKE is an Oakland-based writer and editor, and the coauthor of the *New York Times* bestseller *Foodheim* with Eric Wareheim and *Sundays with Sophie* with Bobby Flay. She has contributed to the *Los Angeles Times*, *San Francisco Chronicle*, *Taste*, *Punch*, and more.